FTCE
PROFESSIONAL EDUCATION

By: Sharon Wynne, M.S.

XAMonline, INC.
Boston

To obtain permission(s) to use the material from this work for any purpose including workshops or seminars, please submit a written request to:

XAMonline, Inc.
25 First Street, Suite 106
Cambridge, MA 02141
Toll Free 1-800-509-4128
Email: info@xamonline.com
Web: www.xamonline.com
Fax: 1-617-583-5552

Library of Congress Cataloging-in-Publication Data

Wynne, Sharon A.
    FTCE Professional Education / Sharon A. Wynne. 3rd ed
    ISBN 978-1-60787-336-5
    1. FTCE Professional Education
    2. Study Guides
    3. FTCE
    4. Teachers' Certification & Licensure
    5. Careers

Disclaimer:

The opinions expressed in this publication are the sole works of XAMonline and were created independently from the National Education Association, Educational Testing Service, or any State Department of Education, National Evaluation Systems or other testing affiliates.

Between the time of publication and printing, state specific standards as well as testing formats and Web site information may change and therefore would not be included in part or in whole within this product. Sample test questions are developed by XAMonline and reflect content similar to that on real tests; however, they are not former test questions. XAMonline assembles content that aligns with state standards but makes no claims nor guarantees teacher candidates a passing score. Numerical scores are determined by testing companies such as NES or ETS and then are compared with individual state standards. A passing score varies from state to state.

Printed in the United States of America   œ-1

FTCE Professional Education
ISBN: 978-1-60787-336-5

Table of Contents

COMPETENCY 9

KNOWLEDGE OF STRATEGIES TO CREATE AND SUSTAIN A SAFE, EFFICIENT, SUPPORTIVE

COMPETENCY 10

KNOWLEDGE OF HOW TO PLAN AND CONDUCT LESSONS IN A VARIETY OF LEARNING ENVIRONMENTS THAT LEAD TO STUDENT OUTCOMES CONSISTENT WITH STATE AND

COMPETENCY 11

KNOWLEDGE OF COLLABORATIVE STRATEGIES FOR WORKING WITH VARIOUS EDUCATION PROFESSIONALS, PARENTS, AND OTHER APPROPRIATE PARTICIPANTS IN THE

COMPETENCY 12

KNOWLEDGE OF STRATEGIES FOR THE IMPLEMENTATION OF TECHNOLOGY IN THE

COMPETENCY 13
KNOWLEDGE OF THE HISTORY OF EDUCATION AND ITS PHILOSOPHICAL AND SOCIOLOGICAL FOUNDATIONS

COMPETENCY 14
KNOWLEDGE OF SPECIFIC APPROACHES, METHODS, AND STRATEGIES APPROPRIATE FOR STUDENTS WITH LIMITED ENGLISH PROFICIENCY

SAMPLE TEST

FTCE
PROFESSIONAL
EDUCATION

SECTION 1
ABOUT XAMONLINE

XAMonline—A Specialty Teacher Certification Company

Created in 1996, XAMonline was the first company to publish study guides for state-specific teacher certification examinations. Founder Sharon Wynne found it frustrating that materials were not available for teacher certification preparation and decided to create the first single, state-specific guide. XAMonline has grown into a company of over 1,800 contributors and writers and offers over 300 titles for the entire PRAXIS series and every state examination. No matter what state you plan on teaching in, XAMonline has a unique teacher certification study guide just for you.

XAMonline—Value and Innovation

We are committed to providing value and innovation. Our print-on-demand technology allows us to be the first in the market to reflect changes in test standards and user feedback as they occur. Our guides are written by experienced teachers who are experts in their fields. And our content reflects the highest standards of quality. Comprehensive practice tests with varied levels of rigor means that your study experience will closely match the actual in-test experience.

To date, XAMonline has helped nearly 600,000 teachers pass their certification or licensing exams. Our commitment to preparation exceeds simply providing the proper material for study—it extends to helping teachers **gain mastery** of the subject matter, giving them the **tools** to become the most effective classroom leaders possible, and ushering today's students toward a **successful future**.

SECTION 2
ABOUT THIS STUDY GUIDE

Purpose of This Guide

Is there a little voice inside of you saying, "Am I ready?" Our goal is to replace that little voice and remove all doubt with a new voice that says, "I AM READY. **Bring it on!**" by offering the highest quality of teacher certification study guides.

Organization of Content

You will see that while every test may start with overlapping general topics, each is very unique in the skills they wish to test. Only XAMonline presents custom content that analyzes deeper than a title, a subarea, or an objective. Only XAMonline presents content and sample test assessments along with **focus statements**, the deepest-level rationale and interpretation of the skills that are unique to the exam.

Title and field number of test
→Each exam has its own name and number. XAMonline's guides are written to give you the content you need to know for the specific exam you are taking. You can be confident when you buy our guide that it contains the information you need to study for the specific test you are taking.

Subareas
→These are the major content categories found on the exam. XAMonline's guides are written to cover all of the subareas found in the test frameworks developed for the exam.

Objectives
→These are standards that are unique to the exam and represent the main subcategories of the subareas/content categories. XAMonline's guides are written to address every specific objective required to pass the exam.

Focus statements
→These are examples and interpretations of the objectives. You find them in parenthesis directly following the objective. They provide detailed examples of the range, type, and level of content that appear on the test questions. **Only XAMonline's guides drill down to this level.**

How Do We Compare with Our Competitors?

XAMonline—drills down to the focus statement level.
CliffsNotes and REA—organized at the objective level
Kaplan—provides only links to content
MoMedia—content not specific to the state test

Each subarea is divided into manageable sections that cover the specific skill areas. Explanations are easy to understand and thorough. You'll find that every test answer contains a rejoinder so if you need a refresher or further review after taking the test, you'll know exactly to which section you must return.

How to Use This Book

Our informal polls show that most people begin studying up to eight weeks prior to the test date, so start early. Then ask yourself some questions: How much do you really know? Are you coming to the test straight from your teacher-education program or are you having to review subjects you haven't considered in ten years? Either way, take a **diagnostic or assessment test** first. Also, spend time on sample tests so that you become accustomed to the way the actual test will appear.

This guide comes with an online diagnostic test of 30 questions found online at *www.XAMonline.com*. It is a little boot camp to get you up for the task and reveal things about your compendium of knowledge in general. Although this guide is structured to follow the order of the test, you are not required to study in that order. By finding a time-management and study plan that fits your life you will be more effective. The results of your diagnostic or self-assessment test can be a guide for how to manage your time and point you toward an area that needs more attention.

After taking the diagnostic exam, fill out the **Personalized Study Plan** page at the beginning of each chapter. Review the competencies and skills covered in that chapter and check the boxes that apply to your study needs. If there are sections you already know you can skip, check the "skip it" box. Taking this step will give you a study plan for each chapter.

Week	Activity
8 weeks prior to test	Take a diagnostic test found at www.XAMonline.com
7 weeks prior to test	Build your Personalized Study Plan for each chapter. Check the "skip it" box for sections you feel you are already strong in. ✗ SKIP IT ☐
6-3 weeks prior to test	For each of these four weeks, choose a content area to study. You don't have to go in the order of the book. It may be that you start with the content that needs the most review. Alternately, you may want to ease yourself into plan by starting with the most familiar material.
2 weeks prior to test	Take the sample test, score it, and create a review plan for the final week before the test.
1 week prior to test	Following your plan (which will likely be aligned with the areas that need the most review) go back and study the sections that align with the questions you may have gotten wrong. Then go back and study the sections related to the questions you answered correctly. If need be, create flashcards and drill yourself on any area that you makes you anxious.

SECTION 3
ABOUT THE FTCE PROFESSIONAL EDUCATION EXAM

What Is the FTCE Professional Education Exam?

The FTCE Professional Education exam is a test of basic pedagogy and professional practices. It is administered by Pearson Education on behalf of the Florida Department of Education.

Often **your own state's requirements** determine whether or not you should take any particular test. The most reliable source of information regarding this is your state's Department of Education. This resource should have a complete list of testing centers and dates. Test dates vary by subject area and not all test dates necessarily include your particular test, so be sure to check carefully.

If you are in a teacher-education program, check with the Education Department or the Certification Officer for specific information for testing and testing timelines. The Certification Office should have most of the information you need.

If you choose an alternative route to certification you can either rely on our web site at *www.XAMonline.com* or on the resources provided by an alternative certification program. Many states now have specific agencies devoted to alternative certification and there are some national organizations as well, for example:

National Association for Alternative Certification
http://www.alt-teachercert.org/index.asp

Interpreting Test Results

Contrary to what you may have heard, the results of the FTCE Professional Education test are not based on time. More accurately, you will be scored on the raw number of points you earn in relation to the raw number of points available. Each question is worth one raw point. It is likely to your benefit to complete as many questions in the time allotted, but it will not necessarily work to your advantage if you hurry through the test.

Follow the guidelines provided by Pearson for interpreting your score. The web site offers a sample test score sheet and clearly explains how/whether the scores are scaled and what to expect if you have an essay portion on your test.

Scores are available approximately 3-4 weeks after the test date and scores will be sent to you and your chosen institution(s).

What's on the Test?

The FTCE Professional Education exam lasts 2.5 hours and consists of 120 multiple-choice questions covering the following content categories: Assessment; Communications; Continuous Improvement; Critical Thinking; Diversity; Ethics; Human Development and Learning; Subject Matter; Learning Environment; Planning; Role of the Teacher; Technology; Foundations of Education; and ESOL.

Question Types

You're probably thinking, enough already, I want to study! Indulge us a little longer while we explain that there is actually more than one type of multiple-choice question. You can thank us later after you realize how well prepared you are for your exam.

1. **Complete the Statement.** The name says it all. In this question type you'll be asked to choose the correct completion of a given statement. For example:

> **The Dolch Basic Sight Words consist of a relatively short list of words that children should be able to:**
>
> A. Sound out
>
> B. Know the meaning of
>
> C. Recognize on sight
>
> D. Use in a sentence

The correct answer is A. In order to check your answer, test out the statement by adding the choices to the end of it.

2. **Which of the Following.** One way to test your answer choice for this type of question is to replace the phrase "which of the following" with your selection. Use this example:

> **Which of the following words is one of the twelve most frequently used in children's reading texts:**
>
> A. There
>
> B. This
>
> C. The
>
> D. An

Don't look! Test your answer. _____ is one of the twelve most frequently used in children's reading texts. Did you guess C? Then you guessed correctly.

3. Roman Numeral Choices. This question type is used when there is more than one possible correct answer. For example:

> **Which of the following two arguments accurately supports the use of cooperative learning as an effective method of instruction?**
> I.   Cooperative learning groups facilitate healthy competition between individuals in the group.
> II. Cooperative learning groups allow academic achievers to carry or cover for academic underachievers.
> III. Cooperative learning groups make each student in the group accountable for the success of the group.
> IV. Cooperative learning groups make it possible for students to reward other group members for achieving.
>
> A. I and II
> B. II and III
> C. I and III
> D. III and IV

Notice that the question states there are **two** possible answers. It's best to read all the possibilities first before looking at the answer choices. In this case, the correct answer is D.

4. Negative Questions. This type of question contains words such as "not," "least," and "except." Each correct answer will be the statement that does **not** fit the situation described in the question. Such as:

> **Multicultural education is not**
> A. An idea or concept
> B. A "tack-on" to the school curriculum
> C. An educational reform movement
> D. A process

Think to yourself that the statement could be anything but the correct answer. This question form is more open to interpretation than other types, so read carefully and don't forget that you're answering a negative statement.

5. Questions that Include Graphs, Tables, or Reading Passages. As always, read the question carefully. It likely asks for a very specific answer and not a broad interpretation of the visual. Here is a simple (though not statistically accurate) example of a graph question:

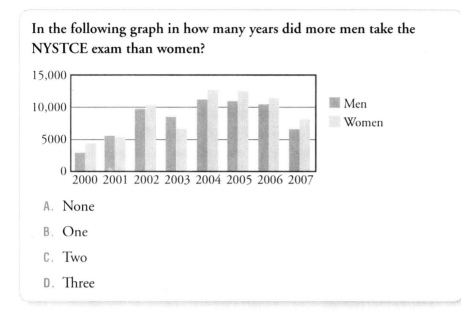

In the following graph in how many years did more men take the NYSTCE exam than women?

A. None

B. One

C. Two

D. Three

It may help you to simply circle the two years that answer the question. Make sure you've read the question thoroughly and once you've made your determination, double check your work. The correct answer is C.

SECTION 4
HELPFUL HINTS

Study Tips

1. You are what you eat. Certain foods aid the learning process by releasing natural memory enhancers called CCKs (cholecystokinin) composed of tryptophan, choline, and phenylalanine. All of these chemicals enhance the neurotransmitters associated with memory and certain foods release memory enhancing chemicals. A light meal or snacks of one of the following foods fall into this category:

• Milk   • Rice   • Eggs   • Fish

• Nuts and seeds   • Oats   • Turkey

The better the connections, the more you comprehend!

2. See the forest for the trees. In other words, get the concept before you look at the details. One way to do this is to take notes as you read, paraphrasing or summarizing in your own words. Putting the concept in terms that are comfortable and familiar may increase retention.

3. Question authority. Ask why, why, why? Pull apart written material paragraph by paragraph and don't forget the captions under the illustrations. For example, if a heading reads *Stream Erosion* put it in the form of a question (Why do streams erode? What is stream erosion?) then find the answer within the material. If you train your mind to think in this manner you will learn more and prepare yourself for answering test questions.

4. Play mind games. Using your brain for reading or puzzles keeps it flexible. Even with a limited amount of time your brain can take in data (much like a computer) and store it for later use. In ten minutes you can: read two paragraphs (at least), quiz yourself with flash cards, or review notes. Even if you don't fully understand something on the first pass, your mind stores it for recall, which is why frequent reading or review increases chances of retention and comprehension.

5. Place yourself in exile and set the mood. Set aside a particular place and time to study that best suits your personal needs and biorhythms. If you're a night person, burn the midnight oil. If you're a morning person set yourself up with some coffee and get to it. Make your study time and place as free from distraction as possible and surround yourself with what you need, be it silence or music. Studies have shown that music can aid in concentration, absorption, and retrieval of information. Not all music, though. Classical music is said to work best

6. Get pointed in the right direction. Use arrows to point to important passages or pieces of information. It's easier to read than a page full of yellow highlights. Highlighting can be used sparingly, but add an arrow to the margin to call attention to it.

The proctor will write the start time where it can be seen and then, later, provide the time remaining, typically fifteen minutes before the end of the test.

7. Check your budget. You should at least review all the content material before your test, but allocate the most amount of time to the areas that need the most refreshing. It sounds obvious, but it's easy to forget. You can use the study rubric above to balance your study budget.

8. The pen is mightier than the sword. Learn to take great notes. A by-product of our modern culture is that we have grown accustomed to getting our information in short doses. We've subconsciously trained ourselves to assimilate information into neat little packages. Messy notes fragment the flow of information. Your notes can be much clearer with proper formatting. *The Cornell Method* is one such format. This method was popularized in *How to Study in College*, Ninth Edition, by Walter Pauk. You can benefit from the method without purchasing an additional book by simply looking up the method online. Below is a sample of how *The Cornell Method* can be adapted for use with this guide.

← 2½" → **Cue Column**	← 6" → **Note Taking Column** 1. Record: During your reading, use the note-taking column to record important points. 2. Questions: As soon as you finish a section, formulate questions based on the notes in the right-hand column. Writing questions helps to clarify meanings, reveal relationships, establish community, and strengthen memory. Also, the writing of questions sets the state for exam study later. 3. Recite: Cover the note-taking column with a sheet of paper. Then, looking at the questions or cue-words in the question and cue column only, say aloud, in your own words, the answers to the questions, facts, or ideas indicated by the cue words. 4. Reflect: Reflect on the material by asking yourself questions. 5. Review: Spend at least ten minutes every week reviewing all your previous notes. Doing so helps you retain ideas and topics for the exam.
↑ 2" ↓	**Summary** After reading, use this space to summarize the notes from each page.

Adapted from How to Study in College, Ninth Edition, by Walter Pauk, ©2008 Wadsworth

Testing Tips

1. **Get smart, play dumb.** Sometimes a question is just a question. No one is out to trick you, so don't assume that the test writer is looking for something other than what was asked. Stick to the question as written and don't overanalyze.

2. **Do a double take.** Read test questions and answer choices at least twice because it's easy to miss something, to transpose a word or some letters. If you have no idea what the correct answer is, skip it and come back later if there's time. If you're still clueless, it's okay to guess. Remember, you're scored on the number of questions you answer correctly and you're not penalized for wrong answers. The worst case scenario is that you miss a point from a good guess.

3. **Turn it on its ear.** The syntax of a question can often provide a clue, so make things interesting and turn the question into a statement to see if it changes the meaning or relates better (or worse) to the answer choices.

4. **Get out your magnifying glass.** Look for hidden clues in the questions because it's difficult to write a multiple-choice question without giving away part of the answer in the options presented. In most questions you can readily eliminate one or two potential answers, increasing your chances of answering correctly to 50/50, which will help out if you've skipped a question and gone back to it (see tip #2).

5. **Call it intuition.** Often your first instinct is correct. If you've been studying the content you've likely absorbed something and have subconsciously retained the knowledge. On questions you're not sure about trust your instincts because a first impression is usually correct.

6. **Graffiti.** Sometimes it's a good idea to mark your answers directly on the test booklet and go back to fill in the optical scan sheet later. You don't get extra points for perfectly blackened ovals. If you choose to manage your test this way, be sure not to mismark your answers when you transcribe to the scan sheet.

7. **Become a clock-watcher.** You have a set amount of time to answer the questions. Don't get bogged down laboring over a question you're not sure about when there are ten others you could answer more readily. If you choose to follow the advice of tip #6, be sure you leave time near the end to go back and fill in the scan sheet.

Do the Drill

No matter how prepared you feel it's sometimes a good idea to apply Murphy's Law. So the following tips might seem silly, mundane, or obvious, but we're including them anyway.

1. **Remember, you are what you eat, so bring a snack.** Choose from the list of energizing foods that appear earlier in the introduction.

2. **You're not too sexy for your test.** Wear comfortable clothes. You'll be distracted if your belt is too tight or if you're too cold or too hot.

3. **Lie to yourself.** Even if you think you're a prompt person, pretend you're not and leave plenty of time to get to the testing center. Map it out ahead of time and do a dry run if you have to. There's no need to add road rage to your list of anxieties.

4. **Bring sharp number 2 pencils.** It may seem impossible to forget this need from your school days, but you might. And make sure the erasers are intact, too.

5. **No ticket, no test.** Bring your admission ticket as well as **two** forms of identification, including one with a picture and signature. You will not be admitted to the test without these things.

6. **You can't take it with you.** Leave any study aids, dictionaries, notebooks, computers, and the like at home. Certain tests **do** allow a scientific or four-function calculator, so check ahead of time to see if your test does.

7. **Prepare for the desert.** Any time spent on a bathroom break **cannot** be made up later, so use your judgment on the amount you eat or drink.

8. **Quiet, Please!** Keeping your own time is a good idea, but not with a timepiece that has a loud ticker. If you use a watch, take it off and place it nearby but not so that it distracts you. And **silence your cell phone**.

To the best of our ability, we have compiled the content you need to know in this book and in the accompanying online resources. The rest is up to you. You can use the study and testing tips or you can follow your own methods. Either way, you can be confident that there aren't any missing pieces of information and there shouldn't be any surprises in the content on the test.

If you have questions about test fees, registration, electronic testing, or other content verification issues please visit *www.fl.nesinc.com*.

Good luck!

Sharon Wynne
Founder, XAMonline

FTCE
PROFESSIONAL
EDUCATION

PERSONALIZED STUDY PLAN

KNOWN MATERIAL/ SKIP IT

PAGE	COMPETENCY AND SKILL	
6	**1: Knowledge of various types of assessment strategies that can be used to determine student levels and needs**	☐
	1.1: Identify measurement concepts, characteristics, and uses of various assessments	☐
	1.2: Interpret assessment data to guide instructional decisions	☐
	1.3: Identify appropriate methods for assessing student learning	☐
	1.4: Identify and sequence learning activities	☐
14	**2: Knowledge of effective communication with students, parents, faculty, other professionals, and the public, including those whose home language is not English**	☐
	2.1: Identify appropriate techniques for leading class discussions	☐
	2.2: Identify ways to correct student errors	☐
	2.3: Identify nonverbal communication strategies that promote student performance	☐
	2.4: Choose effective communication techniques	☐
29	**3: Knowledge of strategies for continuous improvement in professional practices for self and school**	☐
	3.1: Identify experiences that enhance teacher performance and student achievement	☐
	3.2: Identify ways data can be used in teaching practices	☐
32	**4: Knowledge of strategies, materials, and technologies that will promote and enhance critical and creative thinking skills**	☐
	4.1: Identify strategies that foster critical thinking	☐
	4.2: Identify strategies that foster creative thinking	☐
37	**5: Knowledge of cultural, linguistic, and learning style differences and how these differences affect classroom practice and student learning**	☐
	5.1: Identify skills that create a positive learning climate	☐
	5.2: Select strategies that encourage learning about diverse cultural groups	☐
41	**6: Knowledge of the Code of Ethics and Principles of Professional Conduct of the Education Profession in Florida**	☐
	6.1: Apply the Code of Ethics and Principles of Professional Conduct	☐
	6.2: Identify grounds for disciplinary action, the penalties that can be imposed by the Educational Practices Commission against a certificate holder, and the appeals process	☐

PERSONALIZED STUDY PLAN

PERSONALIZED STUDY PLAN

KNOWN MATERIAL/ SKIP IT

PAGE	COMPETENCY AND SKILL	
84	**11: Knowledge of collaborative strategies for working with various education professionals, parents, and other appropriate participants in the continual improvement of educational experiences of students**	☐
	11.1: Identify student behavior indicating possible emotional distress, substance abuse, abuse or neglect, and suicidal tendencies	☐
	11.2: Identify resources and collaborative procedures to meet the needs of all students	☐
	11.3: Identify the rights, responsibilities, and procedures for reporting incidences of abuse or neglect	☐
	11.4: Apply knowledge of the contents of, and the procedures for, maintaining student records	☐
	11.5: Identify the role of teachers on collaborative teams	☐
	11.6: Interpret statewide criterion-referenced assessment data for parents	☐
	11.7: Interpret national norm-referenced assessment data for parents	☐
99	**12: Knowledge of strategies for the implementation of technology in the teaching and learning process**	☐
	12.1: Identify appropriate software to prepare materials, deliver instruction, assess student achievement, and manage classroom tasks	☐
	12.2: Identify appropriate classroom procedures for student use of technology	☐
	12.3: Identify policies for the safe and ethical use of the Internet, networks, and other electronic media	☐
	12.4: Identify strategies for instructing students in research techniques	☐
104	**13: Knowledge of the history of education and its philosophical and sociological foundations**	☐
	13.1: Apply historical, philosophical, and sociological perspectives to contemporary issues in American education	☐
	13.2: Identify contemporary philosophical views on education	☐
108	**14: Knowledge of specific approaches, methods, and strategies appropriate for students with limited English proficiency**	☐
	14.1: Identify characteristics of first and second language acquisition	☐
	14.2: Identify ESOL approaches, methods, and strategies	☐
	14.3: Identify and apply cognitive approaches, multisensory ESOL strategies, and instructional practices	☐

COMPETENCY 1

KNOWLEDGE OF VARIOUS TYPES OF ASSESSMENT STRATEGIES THAT CAN BE USED TO DETERMINE STUDENT LEVELS AND NEEDS

> **SKILL 1.1** Identify measurement concepts, characteristics, and uses of norm-referenced, criterion-referenced, and performance-based assessments

In evaluating school reform for school communities, educators may implement and assess student academic performance using a variety of tools, including norm-referenced, criterion-referenced, and performance-based assessments.

Effective classroom assessment can provide educators with a wealth of information on student performance as well as teacher instructional practices. Student assessment can provide teachers with the data needed to analyze student academic performance and make inferences about the effectiveness of student learning plans, which can foster increased academic achievement and success for students.

Assessment

The process of collecting, quantifying, and qualifying student performance is defined as ASSESSMENT. A comprehensive assessment system must include a diversity of assessment tools such as norm-referenced, criterion-referenced, performance-based, or student-generated alternative assessments, which can measure specific learning outcomes or goals for student achievement.

> **ASSESSMENT:** the process of collecting, quantifying, and qualifying student performance

Norm-referenced assessments

NORM-REFERENCED TESTS (NRT) are used to classify student learners for homogenous groupings based on ability levels or basic skills into a ranking category. In many school communities, NRTs are used to classify students into AP (Advanced Placement), honors, regular, or remedial classes that can significantly impact students' future educational opportunities or success. NRTs are also used by national testing companies such as Iowa Test of Basic Skills (Riverside), Florida Achievement Test (McGraw-Hill), and other major test publishers to test a national sample of students, which are used to develop norms against standard test-takers. Stiggins (1994) states, "Norm-referenced tests (NRT) are designed to highlight achievement differences between and among students to produce a

> **NORM-REFERENCED TESTS (NRT):** used to classify student learners for homogenous groupings based on ability levels or basic skills into a ranking category

dependable rank order of students across a continuum of achievement from high achievers to low achievers."

Educators may use the information from NRTs to provide students with academic learning that accelerates students' skills from the basic level to higher skill applications and thereby enables them to meet the requirements of state assessments and/or core subject expectations. NRT ranking ranges from 1–99 with 25 percent of students scoring in the lower ranking of 1–25 and 25 percent of students scoring in the higher ranking of 76–99. Florida uses a variety of NRTs for student assessments that range from the Iowa Tests of Basic Skills to the California Achievement Test for measuring student learning in reading and math.

Criterion-referenced assessments

CRITERION-REFERENCED ASSESSMENTS examine specific student learning goals and performance compared to a norm group of student learners. According to Bond (1996), "Educators or policy makers may choose to use a criterion-referenced test (CRT) when they wish to see how well students have learned the knowledge and skills which they are expected to have mastered." Many school districts and state legislation use CRTs to ascertain whether schools are meeting national and state learning standards. The latest national educational mandates of No Child Left Behind (NCLB) and Adequate Yearly Progress (AYP) use CRTs to measure student learning, school performance, and school improvement goals as structured accountability expectations in school communities. CRTs are generally used in learning environments to reflect the effectiveness of curriculum implementation and learning outcomes.

> **CRITERION-REFERENCED ASSESSMENTS:** examine specific student learning goals and performance compared to a norm group of student learners

Performance-based assessments

PERFORMANCE-BASED ASSESSMENTS are currently being used in a number of state testing programs to measure the learning outcomes of individual students in subject content areas. Washington State uses performance-based assessments for the Washington Assessment of Student Learning (WASL) in reading, writing, math, and science to measure student-learning performance. It has been a graduation requirement to pass the required state assessment since the class of 2008; this has created high-stakes testing and educational accountability for both students and teachers in meeting the expected skill-based requirements for tenth-grade students taking the test.

> **PERFORMANCE-BASED ASSESSMENTS:** used in a number of state testing programs to measure the learning outcomes of individual students in subject content areas

In today's classrooms, performance-based assessments in core subject areas must have established and specific performance criteria that start with pretesting in the subject area and continue with daily or weekly testing to gauge student progress toward learning goals and objectives. To understand a student's learning is to understand how a student processes information. Effective performance assessments will show the gaps or holes in student learning, which then allows the teacher to focus on providing fillers to bridge nonsequential learning gaps. Typical performance assessments include research papers, oral presentations, class projects, journals, student portfolios, and community service projects.

Summary

With today's emphasis on student accountability, the public and legislature demands for effective teaching and assessment of student learning outcomes will remain of utmost importance.

Performance-based assessments are being used in some areas in the state testing of high school students. Before a state, district, or school community can determine which type of testing is the most effective, there must be a determination of testing outcome expectation, content learning outcome, and a decision as to the effectiveness of the assessment in meeting these learning goals and objectives.

SKILL 1.2 **Interpret assessment data** *(e.g., screening, progress monitoring, diagnostic)* **to guide instructional decisions**

The information contained within student records, teacher observations, and diagnostic testing reports is only as valuable as the individual teacher's ability to comprehend the information. Although the student's cumulative record will contain some or all of this information, it is the responsibility of each teacher to read and interpret the information.

Diagnostic test results are generally uniform and easy to interpret. These reports usually include a scoring guide that tells the teacher how to interpret the information. Teachers must be aware that the scores should be interpreted with some caution, as there are always uncontrollable factors; therefore, test scores alone cannot be the ultimate indicator of a child's ability or learning needs. Many other factors influence these scores, including the rapport the child had with the tester, how the child was feeling when the test was administered, and how the child regarded the value or importance of the test. Therefore, the teacher should regard these scores as a ballpark figure.

When a teacher reads another teacher's observations, it is important to keep in mind that each person brings to an observation certain biases.

When a teacher reads another teacher's observations, it is important to keep in mind that each person brings to an observation certain biases. The reader may also influence the information contained within an observation with his or her own interpretation. When using teacher observations as a basis for designing learning programs, it is necessary to be aware of these shortcomings.

Student records may provide the most assistance in guiding instruction. These records contain information that was gathered over a period of time and may show student growth and progress. They may also contain information provided by several people, including teachers, parents, and other educational professionals. By reading this compilation of information, the teacher may get a more accurate understanding of a student's needs. All of this information is only a stepping stone in determining how a child learns, what a child knows, and what a child needs to know to further his or her education.

> **SKILL 1.3** Identify appropriate methods, strategies, and evaluation instruments for assessing student levels, needs, performance, and learning

Assessment language has been deeply rooted in key terms such as the following:

- Formative: Sets targets for student learning and creates an avenue to provide data on whether students are meeting the targets

- Diagnostic testing: Used to determine students' skill levels and current knowledge

- Normative: Establishes rankings and comparatives of student performances against an established norm of achievement

- Alternative: Nontraditional method of helping students construct responses to problem solving

- Authentic: Real life assessments that are relevant and meaningful in a student's life (for example, calculating the dollar amount for a 20 percent discount on a pair of sneakers)

- Performance-based: Judged according to pre-established standards

- Traditional: Diverse selection of teacher assessments that either come with the textbooks or are directly created from the textbooks

Using Assessment to Adjust Instruction

Assessment skills should be an integral part of teacher training. Teachers need to be able to monitor student learning using pre- and post-assessments of content areas, analyze assessment data in terms of individualized support for students and instructional practice for teachers, and design lesson plans that have measurable outcomes and definitive learning standards. Assessment information should be used to provide performance-based criteria and academic expectations for all students in evaluating whether students have learned the expected skills and content of the subject area.

For example, in an Algebra I class, teachers can use assessment to see whether students have acquired enough prior knowledge to engage in the subject area. If the teacher provides students with a pre-assessment on algebraic expression, he can ascertain whether the lesson plan should be modified to include a pre-algebraic expression lesson unit to refresh student understanding of the content area. If needed, the teacher can then provide quantifiable data to demonstrate the need for additional resources to support student learning. Once the teacher has taught the unit on algebraic expression, a post-assessment test can be used to test student learning, and a mastery exam can be used to test how well students understand and can apply the knowledge to the next unit of math content learning.

Teachers can use assessment data to inform and impact instructional practices by making inferences on teaching methods and gathering clues for student performance. By analyzing the various types of assessments, teachers can gather more definitive information on projected student academic performance. Instructional strategies for teachers would provide learning targets for student behavior, cognitive thinking skills, and processing skills that can be employed to diversify student learning opportunities.

One of the simplest and most efficient ways for the teacher to get to know her students is to conduct an entry survey. This is a record that provides useful background information about the students as they enter a class or school. Collecting information through an entry survey will provide valuable insights into a student's background knowledge and experience. Teachers can customize entry surveys according to the type of information that is valuable to them individually. Some of the information that may be incorporated include the student's name and age, family members, health concerns, special interests, strengths, needs, and fears; parent expectations; languages spoken in the home; what the child likes about school, and so on.

At the beginning of each school term the teacher will likely feel compelled to conduct some informal evaluations in order to obtain a general awareness of his or her students. These informal evaluations should be the result of a learning activity rather than a traditional testing format and may include classroom observations, collections of reading and writing samples, and notations about the students' abilities as demonstrated by classroom discussions and participation. The value of these informal evaluations cannot be underestimated. These evaluations, if utilized effectively, will drive instruction and facilitate learning.

After initial informal evaluations have been conducted and appropriate instruction implemented, teachers will need to fine-tune individual evaluations in order to provide optimum learning experiences. Some of the same types of evaluations that were used to determine initial general learning needs can also be used on an ongoing basis to determine individual learning needs.

It is somewhat more difficult to choose an appropriate evaluation instrument for elementary-aged students than for older students; teachers must be mindful of developmentally appropriate instruments. At the same time, teachers must be cognizant of the information that they wish to attain from a specific evaluation instrument. Ultimately, these two factors—students' developmental stage and the information to be derived—will determine which type of evaluation will be most appropriate and valuable. There are few commercially designed assessment tools that will prove to be as effective as the tool that is constructed by the teacher.

A simple-to-administer, information-rich evaluation of a child's reading strengths and weaknesses is the running reading record. "This technique for recording reading behavior is the most insightful, informative, and instructionally useful assessment procedure you can use for monitoring a child's progress in learning to read" (Traill, 1993). The teacher uses a simple coding system to record what errors and strategies a child uses while reading text out loud. At a later time, the teacher can go back to the record and assess what the child knows about reading and what the teacher still needs to address in an effort to help the student become a better reader.

If the teacher is evaluating a child's writing, it is a good idea to discourage the child from erasing his or her errors and to train the child to cross out errors with a single line so that the teacher can see the process that the student used throughout a writing assignment. This method becomes an important means of getting to know about students' writing.

Mathematics skills can be evaluated informally by observing students as they work at their seats or perform calculations at the board. Teachers can see if the students know basic computation skills, if they understand place value, or if they transpose numbers simply by watching them as they solve computation problems. Some teachers may prefer to administer some basic computation tests to determine a student's mathematical strengths and weaknesses. Although these methods are not as effective or thorough in assessing students, they are quick and easy to administer.

SKILL 1.4 Identify and sequence learning activities that support study skills and test-taking strategies

> *Several studies have been carried out that indicate conclusively that students perform better when they understand what type of test they are going to take and why they are taking the test before they take it.*

Tests are essential instructional tools. They can greatly influence students' learning and should be given due regard for their importance when they are being prepared. Several studies have been carried out that indicate conclusively that students perform better when they understand what type of test they are going to take and why they are taking the test before they take it. If students perceive a test to be important or to have relative significance, they will perform better. In a recent study, students whose teachers informed them as to how their test scores would be used and urged them to put forth their best effort scored higher on the Differential Aptitudes Test than students who did not receive this coaching.

Motivation to perform well on tests begins with the student. The intrinsic motivation is an internal drive by the student who aspires to do his or her best in school. The extrinsic motivation may be as simple as a student wanting to learn a basic mathematical skill to complete a remedial math class, or as complex as a student needing to pass a pre-calculus class to take an AP (Advanced Placement) calculus class during his senior year so that he may gain college credit and enter university as an early admission applicant.

Students will also attain higher test scores if they are familiar with the format of the test. It is important for the student to know whether he will be taking a multiple choice test or an essay test. Being prepared for a specific test format can enhance performance. Teachers can help students boost their test performance by providing them with explicit information in regard to the content of the test.

If the focus is on improving student performance on tests, then students must become familiar with the diversity of test taking formats. Students must understand that there are basic study skills and preparations that maximize student outcomes.

In researching the effects of sleep deprivation on student learning and test-taking, Carlyle Smith, a professor of psychology at Trent University in Ontario, determined that when students are taught a complex logic game of memorization, their performance on the logic game decreased by 30 percent when the students were in a sleep-deprived state on the first night. In testing a second group of volunteers who had been deprived of sleep on a second night and another group given a full three nights' rest, the results were similar in that the sleep-deprived students' performance on the logic game was poorer than the performance of the well-rested students. For students, the best performance for test taking begins with a good night's sleep.

Effective test taking includes an ability to size up testing formats and quickly eliminate incorrect answers from a listing of possible choices. The good news is that a student has a 25 percent chance of getting the correct answer from a choice of four answers and a 50 percent chance once the decoys and incomplete answers have been eliminated so that two answers remain. Knowing how the test is constructed will get a student those better odds.

Objective Tests

Most objective tests will include multiple choice questions, matching, and true/false questions that include a selection of answer choices. The correct answer can be found using a simple process of elimination of decoy of incomplete answers. Helping students review material needed for the tests and providing them sample practice questions will increase student testing performance. Listed below are basic strategies for taking multiple choice tests such as the SAT, ACT, state tests, and class assessment.

- Read the questions and the answers thoroughly

- Look for decoy or partial answers and eliminate them

- Make an educated guess from the answers that remain

- For true/false answers, if any part of the answer given is false, then the entire answer is false, so you have a 50-50 chance of getting a correct response from true/false

- Answer the easy questions first and spend more time on the harder questions

- Listen to your gut instinct on tests; usually your first instinct is correct, but don't be afraid to second guess your gut if you know for a fact that part of the answer that you've chosen has a false component embedded in the answer

Subjective Tests

Subjective tests put the student in the driver's seat. These types of assessments usually consist of short answer questions, essays, or problem-solving questions that involve critical thinking skills and require definitive proof from the short reading passages to support the answer. Sometimes teachers provide rubrics that include assessment criteria for high scoring answers and projects. The bottom line is that studying and preparing for any type of test will produce better student performance on tests.

COMPETENCY 2

KNOWLEDGE OF EFFECTIVE COMMUNICATION WITH STUDENTS, PARENTS, FACULTY, OTHER PROFESSIONALS, AND THE PUBLIC, INCLUDING THOSE WHOSE HOME LANGUAGE IS NOT ENGLISH

SKILL 2.1 **Identify appropriate techniques for leading class discussions** (e.g., listening, identifying relevant information, probing, drawing inferences, summarizing student comments, and redirecting)

The major teaching functions include getting the class under way; providing instruction about what to complete; developing the lesson; managing seat work, homework, and practice; and conducting reviews. All of these functions require teachers to comprehend the aptitude and achievement of students, the appropriateness of subject matter, and the kinds of difficulties students may encounter as they try to learn.

Engaging Students in Lessons

Students' attitudes and perceptions about learning are the most powerful factors influencing academic focus and success. When instructional objectives center on students' interests and are relevant to their lives, effective learning occurs.

Learners must believe that the tasks that they are being asked to perform have some value and that they have both the ability and the resources to perform them. If a student believes a task is unimportant, he will not put much effort into it. Additionally, if a student thinks she lacks the ability or resources to successfully complete a task, even attempting the task becomes too great a risk. Not only must the teacher understand the students' abilities and interests, he must also help students develop positive attitudes and perceptions about learning tasks.

Teachers can enhance student motivation by planning and directing interactive, hands-on learning experiences. Research substantiates that cooperative group projects decrease student behavior problems and increase student on-task behavior. Students who are directly involved with learning activities are more motivated to complete a task to the best of their ability.

Students generally do not realize their own abilities and frequently lack self-confidence. Teachers can instill positive self-concepts in children and thereby enhance their innate abilities by providing certain types of feedback. Such feedback includes attributing students' successes to their effort and specifying what the student did that produced the success. Qualitative comments influence attitudes more than quantitative feedback such as grades.

Despite a teacher's best efforts to provide important and appropriate instruction, there may be times when a teacher is required to teach a concept, skill, or topic that students may perceive as trivial and irrelevant. These tasks can be effectively presented if the teacher exhibits a sense of enthusiasm and excitement about the content. Teachers can help spark the students' interest by providing anecdotes and interesting digressions. Research indicates that as teachers become significantly more enthusiastic, students exhibit increased on-task behavior.

Research indicates that as teachers become significantly more enthusiastic, students exhibit increased on-task behavior.

Teachers must avoid teaching tasks that fit only their own interests and goals and instead design activities that address the students' concerns. In order to do this, it is necessary to have a sense of students' interests and goals. Teachers can do this by conducting student surveys and simply questioning and listening to students. Once this information is obtained, the teacher can link students' interests with classroom tasks.

Student responses

There is great value in giving assignments that meet the individual abilities and needs of students. After instruction, discussion, questioning, and practice have been provided, rather than assigning one task to all students, teachers may ask students to generate tasks that will show their knowledge of the information presented. When students are given choices, they have the opportunity to effectively demonstrate the skills, concepts, or knowledge that they, as individuals, have learned. It has been established that student choice increases student originality, intrinsic motivation, and higher mental processes.

Various studies have shown that learning is increased when the teacher acknowledges and amplifies student responses. This can be even more effective if the teacher takes one student's response and directs it to another student for further comment. When this occurs, the students acquire greater subject matter knowledge. This is due to a number of factors.

One is that the student feels that she is a valuable contributor to the lesson. Another is that all students are forced to pay attention because they never know when they will be called on—a phenomenon known as GROUP ALERT. The teacher achieves group alert by stating the question, pausing to allow the students to process the question and formulate an answer, and then calling on someone to answer. If the teacher calls on someone before stating the question, the rest of the students tune out because they know they are not responsible for the answer.

GROUP ALERT: stating the question, pausing to allow the students to process the question and formulate an answer, and then calling on someone to answer

Teachers are advised to also alert the nonperformers to pay attention because they may be called on to elaborate on the answer. Nonperformers are defined as all the students not chosen to answer.

> If the teacher can ellicit even part of an answer from a lower-achieving student and then move the spotlight off of that student onto another student, the lower-achieving student will be more likely to engage in the class discussion the next time.

The idea of directing one student comment to another student is a valuable tool for engaging the lower-achieving student. If the teacher can ellicit even part of an answer from a lower-achieving student and then move the spotlight off of that student onto another student, the lower-achieving student will be more likely to engage in the class discussion the next time. This is because he was not put on the spot for very long and successfully contributed to the class discussion.

Additionally, the teacher shows acceptance of and gives value to student responses by acknowledging, amplifying, discussing, or restating the comment or question. If you allow a student response, even if it is blurted out, you must acknowledge the student response and tell the student the quality of the response.

For example, the teacher asks, "Is chalk a noun?" During the pause time a student says, "Oh, so my bike is a noun." Without breaking the concentration of the class, the teacher looks to the student, nods, and places his or her index finger to the lips as a signal for the student not to speak out of turn, and then calls on someone to respond to the original question. If the blurted-out response is incorrect or needs further elaboration, the teacher may just hold up his or her index finger as an indication to the student that the class will address the response when the class is finished with the current question.

A teacher acknowledges a student response by commenting on it. For example, the teacher states the definition of a noun and asks for examples of nouns in the classroom. A student responds, "My pencil is a noun." The teacher answers, "Okay, let us list that on the board." By this response and the action of writing "pencil" on the board, the teacher has just incorporated the student's response into the lesson.

A teacher may also amplify the student response through another question directed either to the original student or to another student. For example, the teacher may say, "Okay," giving the student feedback on the quality of the answer, and then add, "What do you mean by 'run' when you say, 'the battery runs the radio'?"

Another way of showing acceptance and value of student response is to discuss the student response. For example, after a student responds, the teacher would say, "Everyone, let's think along that line. What is some evidence that proves what Susie just stated?"

And finally, the teacher may restate the response. For example, the teacher might say, "So you are saying that the seasons are caused by the tilt of the earth. Is this what you meant?"

Thus, a teacher keeps students involved using group alert. Additionally, the teacher shows acceptance and value of student responses by acknowledging, amplifying, discussing, or restating the response. This contributes to maintaining academic focus.

Giving praise

The reason for praise in the classroom is to increase the desirable and eliminate the undesirable. This refers to both conduct and academic focus. Effective praise should be authentic, it should be used in a variety of ways, and it should be low-keyed. ACADEMIC PRAISE is a group of specific statements that give information about the value of the response or its implications. For example, a teacher using academic praise would respond, "That is an excellent analysis of Twain's use of the river in *Huckleberry Finn*," whereas a simple positive response to the same question would be, "That's correct."

The focus of the classroom discussion should be on the subject matter and controlled by teacher-posed questions. When a student response is correct, it is not difficult to maintain academic focus. However, when the student response is incorrect, this task is a little more difficult. The teacher must redirect the discussion to the task at hand and at the same time not devalue the student response. It is risky to respond in a classroom.

> **ACADEMIC PRAISE:** a group of specific statements that give information about the value of the response or its implications

Redirecting student comments

If a student is ridiculed or embarrassed by an incorrect response, the student may shut down and not participate thereafter in classroom discussion. One way to respond to the incorrect answer is to ask the child, "Show me from your book why you think that." This gives the student a chance to correct the answer and redeem himself or herself.

Another possible response from the teacher is to use the answer as a nonexample. For example, after discussing the characteristics of warm-blooded and cold-blooded animals, the teacher asks for some examples of warm-blooded animals. A student raises his or her hand and responds, "A snake." The teacher could then say, "Remember, snakes lay eggs; they do not have live birth. However, a snake is a good nonexample of a mammal."

The teacher then draws a line down the board and under a heading of "nonexample" writes "snake." This action conveys to the child that even though the answer was wrong, it still contributed positively to the class discussion. Notice how the teacher did not digress from the task of listing warm-blooded animals—which, in other words, is maintaining academic focus—and at the same time allowed the student to maintain dignity.

It is more difficult for the teacher to avoid digression when a student poses a nonacademic question. For example, during the classroom discussion of *Romeo and Juliet*, the teacher asks "Who told Romeo Juliet's identity?" A student raises his or her hand and asks, "May I go to the restroom?" The teacher could respond in one of two ways. If the teacher did not feel this was a genuine need, he or she could simply shake his or her head no while repeating the question, "Who told Romeo Juliet's identity?"

If the teacher felt this was a genuine need and could not have waited until a more appropriate time, he or she may hold up the index finger indicating "*just a minute*," and elicit a response to the academic question from another student. Then, during the next academic question's pause-time, the teacher could hand the student the bathroom pass.

Using hand signals and body language to communicate with one student while still talking to the rest of the class demonstrates effective teacher *with-it-ness*. With-it-ness is the behavior that demonstrates to the students that the teacher knows what he or she is doing. In this specific case it is *overlapping with-it-ness*. This is the ability to do two tasks at once. Moreover, it is maintaining academic focus with the class while attending to the needs of the individual student. During the academic day, many nonacademic tasks need to be attended to. If the students learn early on that the teacher is not sidetracked by these interruptions, they will stay on task and greater subject matter acquisition will occur.

The teacher may opt to ignore questions that are posed to throw the class off-task. For example, in response to an academic question, the student asks, "What time does the bell ring?" The teacher may respond by shaking his or her head no and calling on someone else to answer the academic question. Under no circumstances should the student posing the nonacademic question be given an answer. Otherwise, this is rewarding deviant behavior and will result in a loss of academic focus.

Listening

Teachers must avoid teaching tasks that fit their own interests and goals and design activities that address the students' concerns. In order to do this, it is necessary to find out about students and to have a sense of their interests and goals. Teachers can do this by conducting student surveys or simply by questioning and listening to students. Once this information is obtained the teacher can link students' interests with classroom tasks.

Teachers are learning the value of giving assignments that meet the individual abilities and needs of students. After instruction, discussion, questioning, and practice have been provided, rather than assigning one task to all students—teachers are asking students to generate tasks that will show their knowledge of the information presented. Students are given choices and thereby have the opportunity to demonstrate more effectively the skills, concepts, or topics that they as individuals have learned. It has been established that student choice increases student originality, intrinsic motivation, and higher mental processes.

Probing, drawing conclusions, making inferences, and summarizing

The effective teacher uses advanced communication skills such as clarification, probing, drawing conclusions, making inferences, reflection, perception, and summarization as a means to facilitate communication. Teachers who are effective communicators are also good listeners. Teacher behaviors such as eye contact, focusing on student body language, clarifying students' statements, and using "I" messages are effective listeners. The ability to communicate with students, listen effectively, identify relevant and nonrelevant information, and summarize students' messages facilitates establishing and maintaining an optimum classroom learning environment.

The value of teacher observations cannot be underestimated. It is through the use of observations that the teacher is able to informally assess the needs of the students during instruction. These observations will drive the lesson and determine the direction that future lessons will take. Teacher observations also set the pace of instruction and ascertain the flow of both student and teacher discourse. After a lesson is carefully planned, teacher observation is the single most important component of an instructional presentation.

One of the primary behaviors that teachers look for in an observation is on-task behavior. There is no doubt that student time on task directly influences student involvement in instruction and enhances student learning. If the teacher observes that a particular student is not on task, she will change the method of instruction accordingly. She may change from a teacher-directed approach to a more interactive approach. Questioning will increase in order to cull the participation of the students. If appropriate, the teacher will introduce manipulative materials to the lesson. In addition, teachers may switch to a cooperative group activity, thereby removing the responsibility of instruction from the teacher and putting it on the students.

Teachers will also change instructional strategies based on the questions and verbal comments of the students. If the students express any confusion or doubt about the content of the lesson, the teacher will immediately take another approach in presenting the lesson. Sometimes this can be accomplished by simply rephrasing an explanation. At other times, it will be necessary for the teacher to use visual organizers or models for understanding to be clear. Effective teachers are sensitive to the reactions and responses of their students and will almost intuitively know when instruction is valid and when it is not. Teachers will constantly check for student comprehension, attention, and focus throughout the presentation of a lesson.

After the teacher has presented a skill or concept lesson, he or she will allow time for the students to practice the skill or concept. At this point it is essential for the teacher to circulate among the students to check for understanding. If the teacher observes that any of the students did not clearly understand the skill or concept, then she must immediately readdress the issue using another technique or approach.

> **SKILL 2.2** **Identify ways to correct student errors** *(e.g., modeling, providing an explanation or additional information, or asking additional questions)*

Feedback

Teachers are expected to provide feedback to help students learn more. The fear of a low grade alone is not viewed as sufficient to provide students with information as to what was done well and what may need additional work. Students need deeper interaction, particularly as topics become more complex.

How can a teacher provide appropriate feedback so that students will be able to learn from their assessments? First, language should be helpful and constructive. Critical language does not necessarily help students learn. They may become defensive or hurt, and, therefore, they may be more focused on the perceptions than the content. Language that is constructive and helpful will guide students to specific actions and recommendations that would help them improve in the future.

When teachers provide timely feedback, they increase the likelihood that students will reflect on their thought processes as they originally produced the work. When feedback comes weeks after the production of an assignment, the student may not remember what it is that caused him or her to respond in a particular way.

Specific feedback is particularly important. Comments like, "This should be clearer" and "Your grammar needs to be worked on" provide information that students may already know. Commentary that provides very specific actions students could take to make something clearer or to improve her grammar is more beneficial to the student.

Using feedback to promote learning

When teachers provide feedback on a set of assignments, they enhance their students' learning by teaching students how to use the feedback. For example, returning a set of papers can actually do more than provide feedback to students on their initial performance. Teachers can ask students to do additional things to work with their original products, or they can even ask students to take small sections and rewrite based on the feedback. While written feedback will enhance student learning, having students do something with the feedback encourages an even deeper learning and reflection.

Experienced teachers may be reading this and thinking, "When will I ever get the time to provide so much feedback?" Although detailed and timely feedback is important—and necessary—teachers do not have to provide it all the time to increase student learning. They can also teach students how to use scoring guides and rubrics to evaluate their own work, particularly before they hand it in to be graded.

One particularly effective way of doing this is by having students examine models and samples of proficient work. Over the years, teachers should collect samples, remove names and other identifying factors, and show these examples to students so that they understand what is expected of them. Often, when teachers do this, they are surprised to see how much students gain from this in terms of their ability to assess their own performance.

Finally, teachers can help students develop plans for revising and improving upon their work, even if it is not evaluated by the teacher in the preliminary stages. For example, teachers can have students keep track of words they commonly misspell, or they can have students make personal lists of areas on which they feel they need to focus.

Correctives

CORRECTIVES are when the teacher provides an explanation of the error and a correction. For example, the teacher asks the class for a list of verbs. A student answers, "car." The teacher replies, "No, remember, we said a verb shows action. Do you remember what an action is?" The student replies, "Yes, it's doing something." The teacher answers, "Yes, that is correct. Does a car show action?" The student answers, "No." The teacher replies, "No, it doesn't. But what action do we do with a car?" The student answers, "Drive." The teacher responds, "Yes, that is correct. Driving is the action we do with a car, therefore 'drive' is a verb. Could you write 'drive' on the board, please?"

In this example, the student was led to the correct answer through a series of questions. This technique allows the student to contribute positively to the class, even when he or she is unsure of the answer or has the wrong answer. This leads to more student participation, which directly results in greater subject matter retention.

> **CORRECTIVES:** when the teacher provides an explanation of the error and a correction

Redirections

REDIRECTING is when the teacher asks a different student to answer the question or to react to the response. For example, a teacher asks, "What is the topic sentence in this paragraph?" A student replies, "'Tom had a party.'" The teacher asks a second student, "Do you agree with that answer?" The second student replies, "Yes." The teacher then has two choices. He or she may either comment on the appropriateness of the answer, or ask the class if anyone disagrees with the first two students.

This technique keeps the students actively involved in the analysis process rather than having them tune out when they have been given the correct answer. This is because, at this point, the students are not sure if the first answer was correct or not. Therefore, they must stay involved until the entire class has reached a consensus.

This type of probing can lead to more student inferences. E. Abraham, M. Nelson and W. Reynolds explained, in a paper presented to the American Educational Research Association in New York in 1971, that they found this to be true. They examined this type of probing in grades one, six, and eleven during social studies and math classes. They also discovered that the effects were increased in higher-achieving students, which could be partly due to the teacher.

W. B. Dalton noted in the 1971 study that teachers in a normal classroom setting gave more than twice as many positive interactions to their higher-achieving students than they did to their lower-achieving students.

In summary, using correctives and redirects in the classroom leads to greater student involvement. This correlates to higher-level thinking by the students and results in more subject matter retention. The effective teacher is aware of how and when these techniques should be used in the classroom.

SKILL 2.3 Identify nonverbal communication strategies that promote student action and performance

About four to six classroom rules should be posted where students can easily see and read them. These rules should be stated positively and describe specific behaviors so they are easy to understand. Certain rules may also be tailored to meet target goals and IEP requirements of individual students. For example, a new student who has had problems with leaving the classroom may need an individual behavior contract to assist him or her with adjusting to the class rule about remaining in the assigned area. As the students demonstrate the behaviors, the teacher should provide reinforcement and corrective feedback.

Periodic "refresher" practice can be done as needed, for example, after a long holiday or if students begin to "slack off." A copy of the classroom plan should be readily available for substitute use, and the classroom aide should also be familiar with the plan and procedures.

The teacher should clarify and model the expected behavior for the students. In addition to the classroom management plan, a management plan should be developed for special situations, (e.g., fire drills) and transitions (e.g., going to and from the cafeteria). Periodic review of the rules, as well as modeling and practice, may be conducted as needed, such as after an extended school holiday.

Procedures that use social humiliation, withholding of basic needs, pain, or extreme discomfort should never be used in a behavior management plan. Emergency intervention procedures used when the student is a danger to himself or others are not considered behavior management procedures. Throughout the year, the teacher should periodically review the types of interventions being used, assess their effectiveness, and make revisions as needed.

> *Procedures that use social humiliation, withholding of basic needs, pain, or extreme discomfort should never be used in a behavior management plan. Throughout the year, the teacher should periodically review the types of interventions being used, assess their effectiveness, and make revisions as needed.*

Success-Oriented Activities

SUCCESS-ORIENTED ACTIVITIES are tasks that are selected to meet the individual needs of the student. When a student is learning a new skill, tasks should be selected so that the student will be able to earn a high percentage of correct answers during the teacher questioning and seatwork portions of the lesson. Later, the teacher should also include work that challenges students to apply what they have learned and stimulate their thinking.

> **SUCCESS-ORIENTED ACTIVITIES:** tasks that are selected to meet the individual needs of the student

Skill knowledge, strategy use, motivation, and personal interests are all factors that influence individual student success. The student who can't be bothered with reading the classroom textbook may be highly motivated to read the driver's handbook for his or her license or the rulebook for the latest video game. Students who did not master their multiplication tables will likely have problems working with fractions.

In the success-oriented classroom, mistakes are viewed as a natural part of the learning process. The teacher can also show that adults make mistakes by correcting errors without getting unduly upset. The students feel safe to try new things because they know that they have a supportive environment and can correct their mistakes.

Activities that promote student success:

- Are based on useful, relevant content that is clearly specified and organized for easy learning

- Allow sufficient time to learn the skill and are selected for their high rate of success

- Allow students the opportunity to work independently, self-monitor, and set goals

- Provide for frequent monitoring and corrective feedback

- Include collaboration in group activities or peer teaching

Students with learning problems often attribute their successes to luck or ease of the task. Their failures are often blamed on their supposed lack of ability, difficulty of the task, or the fault of someone else. Successful activities, attribution retraining, and learning strategies can help these students discover that they can become independent learners. When the teacher communicates the expectation that the students can be successful learners and chooses activities that will help them be successful, achievement is increased.

Progressing from Directed to Self-Directed Activity

Learning progresses in stages from initial acquisition, when the student requires a lot of teacher guidance and instruction, to adaptation, where the student is able to apply what he or she has learned to new situations outside of the classroom. As students progress through the stages of learning, the teacher gradually decreases the amount of direct instruction and guidance. The teacher is slowly encouraging the student to function more independently.

As students progress through the stages of learning, the teacher gradually decreases the amount of direct instruction and guidance and encourages the student to function independently. The ultimate goal of the learning process is to teach students how to be independent and apply their knowledge.

See also Skill 9.1

STAGES OF LEARNING ACQUISITION		
State	**Teacher Activity**	**Emphasis**
Initial Acquisition	Provide rationale Guidance Demonstration Modeling Shaping Cueing	Errorless learning Backward chaining (working from the final product backward through the steps) Forward chaining (proceeding through the steps to a final product)
Advanced Acquisition	Feedback Error correction Specific directions	Criterion evaluation Reinforcement and reward for accuracy
Proficiency	Positive reinforcement Progress monitoring Teach self-management Increased teacher expectations	Increase speed or performance to the automatic level with accuracy Set goals Self-management
Maintenance	Withdraw direct reinforcement Retention and memory Overlearning Intermittent schedule of reinforcement	Maintain high level of performance Mnemonic techniques Social and intrinsic reinforcement
Generalization	Corrective feedback	Perform skill in different times and places
Adaptation	Stress independent problem solving	Independent problem-solving methods No direct guidance or direct instruction

Adapt for Transitions

Transition refers to changes in class activities that involve movement. Examples are:

- Breaking from large group instruction into small groups for learning centers and small-group instructions

- Moving from classroom to lunch, to the playground, or to elective classes

- Finishing reading at the end of one period and getting ready for math the next period

- Emergency situations such as fire drills

Successful transitions are achieved by using proactive strategies. Early in the year, the teacher pinpoints the transition periods in the day and anticipates possible behavior problems, such as students habitually returning late from lunch. After identifying possible problems with the environment or the schedule, the teacher plans proactive strategies to minimize or eliminate those problems.

Proactive planning also gives the teacher the advantage of being prepared, addressing behaviors before they become problems, and incorporating strategies into the classroom management plan right away. Transition plans can be developed for each type of transition so that the expected behaviors for each situation taught are directly to the students. Some examples might include:

- **Identify the specific behaviors needed for the type of transition:** For example, during a fire drill, students must quickly leave the classroom, walk quietly as a group to the designated exit, proceed to the assigned waiting area, stay with the group, wait for the teacher to receive the all-clear signal, walk quickly and quietly back to the classroom with the group, and reenter the classroom and return to the seat.

  Transition to the cafeteria has a similar walking procedure, but is different in that cafeteria behavior involves waiting in line for food without cutting, pushing, or bothering others in line; leaving the table area clean and neat; putting trays in the designated area; and perhaps sitting at an assigned table. For each situation, the teacher needs to decide what the student will be expected to do, as well as what possible problems to expect.

- **Develop a set of expectations and teach them to the students:** The expected behaviors should be written in a positive, specific language. Establish a rationale for the rules and provide an explanation of the rules. Provide corrective feedback and reinforcement to the students who demonstrate knowledge of the rules.

- **Model the appropriate behavior:** Guide the students through the procedures and give reinforcement to those who correctly model the behavior.

- **Have the students practice the behaviors independently:** As students practice behaviors, continue corrective feedback and reinforcement. Certain situations, like fire drills, will not be practiced daily, but students will have daily opportunities to demonstrate appropriate transition behavior in and out of class.

Nonverbal Communication

The PERFORMANCE MEASUREMENT SYSTEM DOMAINS defines body language as teachers' facial or other body behavior that express interest, excitement, joy, and positive personal relations; boredom, sadness, dissatisfaction, or negative personal relations; or no clear message at all.

The effective teacher communicates nonverbally with students by using positive body language, expressing warmth, concern, acceptance, and enthusiasm. Effective teachers augment their instructional presentations by using positive nonverbal communication such as smiles, open body posture, movement, and eye contact with students. The energy and enthusiasm of the effective teacher can be amplified through positive body language.

> **PERFORMANCE MEASUREMENT SYSTEM DOMAINS:** defines body language as teachers' facial or other body behavior that express interest, excitement, joy, and positive personal relations; boredom, sadness, dissatisfaction, or negative personal relations; or no clear message at all

Increasing On-Task Behavior

Many factors contribute to student on-task behavior, including student interest in the content, student ability, student attitude, and student needs. Teacher behavior can impact student behavior just as strongly as any other factor. It is imperative that teachers use strategies that encourage and maintain on-task behavior. They must also be aware that they alone may be responsible for motivating students.

A natural way to reinforce on-task behavior is for the teacher to plan activities that reflect children's interests and build lessons based on children's ideas. Teachers guide students through lessons by responding to their questions and ideas, engaging them in conversation, and challenging their thinking.

Once a child-centered foundation has been established for presenting a lesson, the teacher must concentrate on maintaining student focus. To some degree teachers can rely on students' internal motivation to acquire competence. This internal motivation can be greatly affected by the teacher's attitude and enthusiasm. The teacher is a vital role model for promoting student motivation.

Questioning can help maintain focus, direct academic discussions, and create interactive instruction. Questioning can also reinforce content and sustain both on-task behavior and student motivation. Asking questions is a significant part of the instructional process and is most effective when it includes both simple comprehension questions and complex higher-order thinking questions.

SKILL 2.4 Choose effective communication techniques for conveying high expectations for student learning

Effective teachers are well versed in the areas of cognitive development, which is crucial to presenting ideas and/or materials to students at a level appropriate to their developmental maturity. Effective teachers have the ability to use nonverbal and verbal patterns of communications that focus on age-appropriate instructions and materials.

Consistent with the Piagean theory of cognitive development, younger children (below age eight) lack language competencies that would allow them to solve complicated problems. Educational instructions and information should be saturated with simplified language to compensate for the limited language competencies of younger children. In contrast, older children (age eight and older) have developed a greater ability to understand language and therefore are capable of solving complex problems.

As the classroom environment becomes increasingly populated with students of differing cognitive, social, and emotional development levels as well as various cultural backgrounds, the teacher must rise to the challenge of presenting ideas and materials appropriate for a diverse group of students. Additionally, materials and ideas must be organized, sequenced, and presented to students in a manner that is consistent with the basic principles of the English language and in a manner relevant to students as a whole.

Students are likely to achieve at a higher level when they know what they are expected to learn. Besides telling the students what they are going to learn, teachers may choose to use advance organizers that include visual motivations such as outlines, graphs, and models. This practice is especially valuable to the visual learner and is a motivational factor for most students.

Specific questions asked at the beginning of a lesson can also help students focus on the content and be more attentive to instruction. Once the lesson is underway, it is further developed by additional questions as well as explanations, checking understanding, making transitions from one topic to another, and sometimes engaging in practice. Teachers who clearly explain difficult points during a lesson and then analyze problems utilizing questioning techniques with the students are more effective than those who do not.

COMPETENCY 3

KNOWLEDGE OF STRATEGIES FOR CONTINUOUS IMPROVEMENT IN PROFESSIONAL PRACTICES FOR SELF AND SCHOOL

SKILL 3.1 Identify professional development experiences that will enhance teacher performance and improve student achievement

Professional development opportunities for teacher performance improvement or enhancement in instructional practices are essential for creating comprehensive learning communities.

In order to promote the vision, mission, and action plans of school communities, teachers must be given toolkits to maximize instructional performances. The development of student-centered learning communities that foster the academic capacities and learning synthesis for all students should be the fundamental goal of professional development for teachers.

The level of professional development may include traditional district workshops that enhance instructional expectations for teachers or the more complicated multiple day workshops given by national and state educational organizations. Most workshops on the national and state level provide clock hours that can be used to renew certifications for teachers every five years. Typically, 150 clock hours is the standard certification number needed to provide a five-year certification renewal, so teachers must attend and complete paperwork for a diversity of workshops that range from one to fifty clock hours according to the timeframe of the workshops.

Florida requires districts and schools to provide in-service professional development opportunities for teachers during the school year dealing with district objectives/expectations and relevant workshops or classes that can enhance the teaching practices for teachers. Clock hours are provided with each class or workshop and the type of professional development being offered to teachers determines clock hours. Each year, schools are required to report the number of workshops, along with the participants attending the workshops, to the Superintendent's office for filing. Teachers collecting clock hour forms are required to file the forms to maintain certification eligibility and job eligibility.

Research by the National Association of Secondary Principals,' "Breaking Ranks II: Strategies for Leading High School Reform" created the following multiple listing of educational practices needed for expanding the professional development opportunities for teachers:

- Interdisciplinary instruction between subject areas

- Identification of individual learning styles to maximize student academic performance

- Training teachers in understanding and applying multiple assessment formats and implementations in curriculum and instruction

- Looking at multiple methods of classroom management strategies

- Providing teachers with national, federal, state, and district curriculum expectations and performance outcomes

- Identifying the school communities' action plan of student learning objectives and teacher instructional practices

- Helping teachers understand how to use data to impact student learning goals and objectives

- Teaching teachers on how to disaggregate student data in improving instruction and curriculum implementation for student academic equity and access

- Develop leadership opportunities for teachers to become school and district trainers to promote effective learning communities for student achievement and success

In promoting professional development opportunities for teachers that enhance student achievement, the bottom line is that teachers must be given the time to complete workshops at no or minimal cost. School and district budgets must include financial resources to support and encourage teachers to engage in mandatory and optional professional development opportunities that create a "win-win" learning experience for students.

Whether a teacher is using criterion-referenced, norm-referenced, or performance-based data to inform and impact student learning and achievement, the more important objective is ensuring that teachers know how to effectively use the data to improve and reflect upon existing teaching instructions. The goal of identifying ways for teachers to use the school data is simple: "Is the teacher's instructional practice improving student learning goals and academic success?"

School data can include demographic profiling, cultural and etnhic academic trends, state and/or national assessments, portfolios, academic subject pre- and post-test assessment and weekly assessments, projects, and disciplinary reports. By looking at trends and discrepancies in school data, teachers can ascertain whether they are meeting the goals and objectives of the state, national, and federal mandates for school improvement reform and curriculum implementation.

Assessments can be used to motivate students to learn and shape the learning environment to provide learning stimulation that optimizes student access to learning. Butler and McMunn (2006) have shown that factors that help motivate students to learn are:

- Involving students in their own assessment

- Matching assessment strategies to student learning

- Consider thinking styles and using assessments to adjust the classroom environment in order to enhance student motivation to learn

Teachers can shape the way students learn by creating engaging learning opportunities that promote student achievement.

SKILL Identify ways for using data from learning environments as a basis 3.2 for exploring and reflecting upon teaching practices

According to Florida Teacher Certification mandates under code 6A-5.065, the first teacher-accomplished practice for effective teachers is assessment, which is further categorized on three levels: accomplished, professional, and pre-professional, as outlined below:

Accomplished practice one—Assessment:

1. Accomplished level: The accomplished teacher uses assessment strategies (traditional and alternate) to assist the continuous development of the learner.

2. Professional level: The professional teacher continually reviews and assesses data gathered from a variety of sources. These sources can include, but shall not be limited to, pre-tests, standardized tests, portfolios, anecdotal records, case studies, subject area inventories, cumulative records, and student services information. The professional teacher develops the student's instructional plan to meet cognitive, social, linguistic, cultural, emotional, and physical needs.

3. Pre-professional level: The pre-professional teacher collects and uses data gathered from a variety of sources. These sources will include both traditional and alternate strategies. Furthermore, the teacher can identify and match the student's instructional plan with their cognitive, social, linguistic, cultural, emotional, and physical needs

See also Skill 3.1

COMPETENCY 4
KNOWLEDGE OF STRATEGIES, MATERIALS, AND TECHNOLOGIES THAT WILL PROMOTE AND ENHANCE CRITICAL AND CREATIVE THINKING SKILLS

SKILL 4.1 Identify a variety of instructional strategies, materials, and technologies that foster critical thinking

Teachers should have a toolkit of instructional strategies at their disposal. Various materials and technologies should be utilized to encourage problem solving and critical thinking about subject content. Within each curriculum chosen by a district comes an expectation that students will master both benchmarks and standards of various learning skills. There is an established level of academic performance and proficiency in public schools that students are required to master in today's classrooms.

Research of national and state standards indicates that there are additional benchmarks and learning objectives in the subject areas of science, foreign language, English language arts, history, art, health, civics, economics, geography, physical education, mathematics, and social studies that students are required to master in state assessments (Marzano & Kendall, 1996).

A critical thinking skill is a skill target that teachers use to help students develop and sustain learning within specific subject areas and so that it then can be applied to other subject areas. For example, when learning to understand algebraic concepts in solving a math word problem on how much fencing material is needed to build a fence around a backyard area that is 8' x 12', a math student must understand the order of numerical expression to simplify algebraic expressions.

Teachers can provide instructional strategies that show students how to group the fencing measurements into an algebraic word problem that, with minor addition, subtraction, and multiplication, can produce a simple number equal to the amount of fencing materials needed to build the fence.

Students use basic skills to understand text, such as a reading passage, a math word problem, or directions for a project. However, students apply critical thinking skills to fully comprehend how what was read could be applied to their own life, how to make comparatives, or what choices could be made based on the factual information given. Teachers are instrumental in helping students use these higher-order thinking skills in everyday activities.

Examples of these types of skills may include:

- Analyzing bills for overcharges
- Comparing shopping ads or catalogue deals
- Finding the main idea from readings
- Applying what's been learned to new situations
- Gathering information or data from a diverse array of sources to plan a project
- Following a sequence of directions
- Looking for cause and effect relationships
- Comparing and contrasting information in synthesizing information

Attention to learner needs during planning is foremost and includes identification of what the students already know or need to know; matching learner needs with instructional elements such as content, materials, activities, and goals; and determining whether students have performed at an acceptable level, following instruction.

Moving through a Taxonomy

Since most teachers want their educational objectives to include higher-level thinking skills, teachers need to direct students toward these higher levels using taxonomy, such as Bloom's. Questioning is an effective tool to build up students to these higher levels.

Low-order questions are useful to begin the process. They ensure that the student is focused on the required information and understands what needs to be included in the thinking process. For example, if the objective is for students to be able to read and understand the story "Goldilocks and the Three Bears," the teacher may wish to begin with low-order questions ("What are some things Goldilocks did while in the bears' home?" [Knowledge] or "Why didn't Goldilocks like the Papa Bear's chair?" [Analysis]).

Through a series of questions, the teacher can move the students toward the top of the taxonomy. For example, the teacher could ask, "If Goldilocks had come to your house, what are some things she may have used?" [Application], "How might the story have differed if Goldilocks had visited the three fishes?" [Synthesis], or "Do you think Goldilocks was good or bad? Why?" [Evaluation]. Through questioning, the teacher can control the thinking process of the class. As students become more involved in the discussion, they are systematically being led toward higher levels of thinking.

The ability to create a personal charting of students' academic and emotional growth using performance-based assessment and individualized portfolios becomes a toolkit for both students and teachers. Teachers can use semester portfolios to help gauge student academic progress and personal growth.

Using graphic organizers and concept web guides, which center around a concept and then applying the concept, is an instructional strategy teachers can use to guide students into further inquiry of the subject matter.

Helping students become effective note-takers and teaching different perspectives for spatial techniques is a proactive teacher strategy to help create a visual learning environment where art and visualization become natural art forms for learning.

In today's computer environment, students must understand that computers cannot replace the creative thinking and skill application of the human mind.

In the Florida Teacher Certification Standards, code 6A-5.065, critical thinking is the fourth assessment criteria for effective teacher performance on the three levels below:

Accomplished practice four—Critical Thinking:

1. Accomplished level: The accomplished teacher uses appropriate techniques and strategies that promote and enhance critical, creative, and evaluative thinking capabilities of students.

2. Professional level: The professional teacher will use a variety of performance assessment techniques and strategies that measure higher-order thinking skills in students and that can provide realistic projects and problem solving activities, which will enable all students to demonstrate their ability to think creatively.

3. Pre-professional level: The pre-professional teacher is acquiring performance assessment techniques and strategies that measure higher-order thinking skills in students and is building a repertoire of realistic projects and problem-solving activities designed to assist all students in demonstrating their ability to think creatively.

SKILL 4.2 Identify a variety of instructional strategies, materials, and technologies resources that foster creative thinking

Teachers who combine diversity in instructional practices with engaging and challenging curriculum and the latest advances in technology can create the ultimate learning environment for creative thinking and continuous learning for students. Teachers who are innovative and creative in instructional practices are able to model and foster creative thinking in their students. Encouraging students to maintain journals or portfolios of their valued work from projects and/or assignments will allow students to track a variety of their creative endeavors in a filing format that can be treasured throughout the educational journey.

When teachers are very deliberate about the questions they use with their students, amazing things in the classroom can happen. Most of us remember questions at the end of the chapter in a textbook, or we remember quiz or test questions. While these potentially have value, they are useless if the questions are not crafted well, the purposes for the questions are not defined, and/or the methods by which students will answer the questions are not engaging.

Keep in mind that "good questioning" does not always imply that there are correct answers. "Good questioning" usually implies that teachers are encouraging deep reflection and active thinking in students. In general, we can say that through questioning, we want students to take risks, solve problems, recall facts, and demonstrate understanding.

When we say that we want students to take risks, we mean that we want them to try out various answers and possibilities. By answering a risk-taking question, students experiment with their academic voices.

Problem-solving questions provoke thought and encourage students to think of questions as ways of framing problems, not indicators that every problem can be solved.

Even though factual recall questions should not be overused, it is important to teach students how to comprehend reading, speech, film, or other media. It is also important that students remember certain facts—and questioning can bring on small levels of stress that potentially trigger memory. However, realize that stress may be very upsetting for some students, and such questions, particularly in public settings, may be inappropriate.

Teachers using manipulatives can help students use their skills in the area of visual processing. Allowing students to journal can help them understand their own learning. Providing avenues for students to present their understandings to the class using posters and/or presentations can be a powerful creative method of teaching and learning.

Finally, by questioning students, we see how much they know. Questioning can be done in a variety of formats. For example, we can question students out loud with a whole class. Teachers should refrain from calling on students too often, but occasionally it is an effective technique. Wait time is particularly important; when asking a question, a teacher should not assume that nobody will answer it if a couple seconds have elapsed. Often wait time encourages some students to answer, or it allows all students time to think about the question. Questioning can also take place in small groups or on paper.

In the Florida Teacher Certification Standards, code 6A-5.065, technology is an assessment criteria for effective teacher performance on the three levels below:

Accomplished practice twelve—Technology:

1. Accomplished level: The accomplished teacher uses appropriate technology in teaching and learning processes.

2. Professional level: The professional teacher uses technology (as appropriate) to establish an atmosphere of active learning with existing and emerging technologies available at the school site. She or he provides students with opportunities to use technology to gather and share information with others and facilitates access to the use of electronic resources.

3. Pre-professional level: The pre-professional teacher uses technology as available at the school site and as appropriate to the learner. She or he provides students with opportunities to actively use technology and facilitates access to the use of electronic resources. The teacher also uses technology to manage, evaluate, and improve instruction.

COMPETENCY 5

KNOWLEDGE OF CULTURAL, LINGUISTIC, AND LEARNING STYLE DIFFERENCES AND HOW THESE DIFFERENCES AFFECT CLASSROOM PRACTICE AND STUDENT LEARNING

SKILL 5.1 Identify instructional and interpersonal skills and classroom practices that encourage innovation and create a positive learning climate for all students

A positive self-concept for a child or adolescent is very important; in terms of the students' ability to learn and to be an integral member of society, self-concept and interpersonal skills provide the foundation upon which all learning is based. If students think poorly of themselves or have sustained feelings of inferiority, they may not be able to optimize their potential for learning. It is therefore part of the teacher's task to ensure that each student develops a positive self-concept.

A positive self-concept does not imply feelings of superiority, perfection, or competence/efficacy. Instead, a positive self-concept involves self-acceptance as a person, liking oneself, and having a proper respect for oneself. The teacher who encourages these qualities has contributed to the development of a positive self-concept in students.

Teachers can take a number of different approaches to enhancing the self-concept of students. One such scheme is called the process approach, which proposes a three-phase model for teaching. This model includes a sensing function, a transforming function, and an acting function. These three phases can be simplified into the words by which the model is usually given: reach, touch, and teach.

1. The sensing, or perceptual, function: Incorporates information or stimuli in an intuitive manner.

2. The transforming function: Conceptualizes abstracts, evaluates, and provides meaning and value to perceived information.

3. The acting function: Chooses actions from several different alternatives to be set forth overtly.

The process model may be applied to almost any curricular field.

An approach that aims directly at the enhancement of self-concept is designated as INVITATIONAL EDUCATION. According to this approach, teachers and their behaviors may be inviting or they may be disinviting. Inviting behaviors enhance self-concept among students, while disinviting behaviors diminish self-concept.

Disinviting behaviors include those that demean students, as well as those that may be chauvinistic, sexist, condescending, thoughtless, or insensitive to student feelings. Inviting behaviors are the opposite of these and are characterized by teachers who act with consistency and sensitivity. Inviting teacher behaviors reflect an attitude of doing with rather than doing to. Students are invited or disinvited depending on the teacher behaviors.

Invitational teachers exhibit the following skills (Biehler and Snowman, 394):

- Reaching each student (learning names, having one-to-one contact)

- Listening with care (picking up subtle cues)

- Being real with students (providing only realistic praise, "coming on straight")

- Being real with oneself (honestly appraising your own feelings and disappointments)

- Inviting good discipline (showing students you have respect in personal ways)

- Handling rejection (not taking lack of student response in personal ways)

- Inviting oneself (thinking positively about oneself)

Cooperative Learning

Cooperative learning situations, as practiced in today's classrooms, grew out of research conducted by several groups in the early 1970s. Cooperative learning situations can range from very formal applications such as Student Teams Achievement Divisions (STAD) and Cooperative Integrated Reading and Composition (CIRC) to less formal groupings known variously as group investigation, learning together, or discovery groups. Cooperative learning as a general term is now firmly recognized and established as a teaching and learning technique in American schools.

Since cooperative learning techniques are so widely diffused in the schools, it is necessary to orient students in the skills by which cooperative learning groups can operate smoothly. Students who cannot interact constructively with other students will not be able to take advantage of the learning opportunities provided by the cooperative learning situations and will furthermore deprive their fellow students of the opportunity for cooperative learning.

These skills form the hierarchy of cooperation in which students first learn to work together as a group, so they may then proceed to levels at which they can engage in simulated conflict situations. This cooperative setting allows different points of view to be constructively entertained.

SKILL 5.2 Select materials and strategies that encourage learning about diverse cultural groups

Effective teaching and learning for students begins with teachers who can demonstrate sensitivity for diversity in teaching and relationships within school communities. Student portfolios should include work with a multicultural perspective. Teachers also need to include diverse cultural resources in their curriculum and instructional practices.

Exposing students to culturally sensitive room decorations or posters that show positive and inclusive messages is one way to demonstrate inclusion of multiple cultures. Teachers should also continuously make cultural connections that are relevant and empowering for all students while communicating academic and behavioral expectations. Cultural sensitivity is communicated beyond the classroom with parents and community members to establish and maintain relationships.

Diversity can be further defined as:

- Differences among learners, classroom settings, and academic outcomes

- Biological, sociological, ethnic, socioeconomic, and psychological needs, as well as learning modalities and styles, among learners

- Differences in classroom settings that promote learning opportunities such as collaborative, participatory, and individualized learning groupings

- Expected learning outcomes that are theoretical, affective, and cognitive for students

Teachers should establish a classroom climate that is culturally respectful and engaging for students. In a culturally sensitive classroom, teachers maintain equity and fairness in student interactions and curriculum implementation. Assessments include cultural responses and perspectives that become further learning opportunities for students. Other artifacts that could reflect teacher/student sensitivity to diversity might consist of:

- Student portfolios reflecting multicultural/multiethnic perspectives

- Journals and reflections from field trips or guest speakers from diverse cultural backgrounds

- Printed materials and wall displays from multicultural perspectives
- Parent/guardian letters in a variety of languages reflecting cultural diversity
- Projects that include cultural history and diverse inclusions
- Disaggregated student data reflecting cultural groups
- Classroom climate of professionalism that fosters diversity and cultural inclusion

The encouragement of diversity education allows teachers a variety of opportunities to expand their experiences with students, staff, community members, and parents from culturally diverse backgrounds. These experiences can be proactively applied to promote cultural diversity inclusion in the classroom. Teachers are able to engage and challenge students to develop and incorporate their own diversity skills in building character and relationships with cultures beyond their own. In changing the thinking patterns of students to become more culturally inclusive, teachers are supporting the globalization.

The Florida Teacher Standard Code 6A-5.065 shown below further exemplifies the importance of diversity in the classroom.

Accomplished practice five—Diversity

1. Accomplished level: The accomplished teacher uses teaching and learning strategies that reflect each student's culture, learning styles, special needs, and socioeconomic background.

2. Professional level: The professional teacher establishes a risk-taking environment that accepts and fosters diversity. The teacher must demonstrate knowledge of varied cultures by practices such as conflict resolution, and mediation, and creating a climate of openness, inquiry, and support.

3. Pre-professional level: The pre-professional teacher establishes a comfortable environment that accepts and fosters diversity. The teacher must demonstrate knowledge and awareness of varied cultures. The teacher creates a climate of openness, inquiry, and support by practicing strategies as acceptance, tolerance, resolution, and mediation.

COMPETENCY 6
KNOWLEDGE OF THE CODE OF ETHICS AND PRINCIPLES OF PROFESSIONAL CONDUCT OF THE EDUCATION PROFESSION IN FLORIDA

SKILL 6.1 Apply the Code of Ethics and Principles of Professional Conduct to realistic professional and personal situations

Florida Code of Ethics—Education Profession 6B-1.001

The Florida Code of Ethics for teachers is extensive in both its professional and personal expectations for teachers within the classroom. All codes are taken directly from the state code of ethics and applied to realistic personal and professional situations in the classroom.

> *The educator values the worth and dignity of every person, the pursuit of truth, devotion to excellence, acquisition of knowledge, and the nurture of democratic citizenship. Essential to the achievement of these standards are the freedoms to learn and to teach and the guarantee of equal opportunity for all.*

The ultimate goal of teachers when they enter the profession of teaching is to provide a comprehensive education for all students by providing challenging curriculum and setting high expectations for learning. In an ideal classroom, the mechanisms for providing the perfect teaching climate and instruction are the norm and not the exception. Given the diversity of learners, the reality is that teachers are confronted with classrooms that are infused with management issues and a significant variety of differentiated learning needs.

Researchers have shown that for new teachers entering the profession, the two greatest obstacles are dealing with increasing behavioral issues in the classroom and dealing with students who are minimally engaged in their own learning process. The goal of teachers is to maintain a toolkit of resources to be able to deal with the ever-changing landscape of learners and classroom environments.

> *The educator's primary professional concern will always be for the student and for the development of the student's potential. The educator will therefore strive for professional growth and will seek to exercise the best professional judgment and integrity.*

In a student-centered learning environment, the goal is to provide the best opportunity for academic success for all students. Integrating the developmental patterns of physical, social, and academic norms for students will provide individual learners with student learning plans that are individualized and specific to their skill levels and needs.

Teachers who effectively develop and maximize a student's potential will use pre- and post-assessments to gather comprehensive data on the existing skill level of the student, then plan and adapt the curriculum to address student skills. Maintaining communication with the student and parents will provide a community approach to learning where all stakeholders are included to maximize student-learning growth.

> *Aware of the importance of maintaining the respect and confidence of one's colleagues, of students, of parents, and of other members of the community, the educator strives to achieve and sustain the highest degree of ethical conduct.*

The ethical conduct of an educator has undergone extensive scrutiny in today's classrooms. Teachers are bound by intense rules and regulations to maintain the highest degree of professional conduct in the classroom. Recent court cases in Florida have examined ethical violations of teachers engaged in improper communication and abuse with students, along with teachers engaged in drug violations and substance abuse in classrooms. It is imperative that teachers educating today's young people have the highest regard for professionalism and be proper role models for students in and out of the classroom.

SKILL 6.2 Identify statutory grounds and procedures for disciplinary action, the penalties that can be imposed by the Educational Practices Commission against a certificate holder, and the appeals process available to the individual

The Florida Code of Professional Conduct for Teachers contains a number of obligations that are intended to protect both the teacher and the student. Potential penalties for educators who violate the professional codes include permanent revocation or suspension of their certification.

It is important that teachers understand and take seriously their professional roles as certified employees of the state of Florida. Creating a safe learning environment and protecting students from any conditions that could be potentially harmful or cause degradation is the first obligation teachers have to students. Being a role model that exemplifies good character and ethical professionalism are the next principles teachers must maintain in order to avoid potential disciplinary action or certificate revocation. The conditions of employment for teachers in Florida follow.

6B-1.006 Principles of Professional Conduct for the Education Profession in Florida

1. The following disciplinary rule shall constitute the Principles of Professional Conduct for the Education Profession in Florida.

2. Violation of any of these principles shall subject the individual to revocation or suspension of the individual educator's certificate, or the other penalties as provided by law.

3. Obligation to the student requires that the individual:

   - Shall make reasonable efforts to protect the student from conditions harmful to learning and/or to the student's mental and/or physical health and/or safety.

   - Shall not withhold information regarding a position from an applicant or misrepresenting an assignment or conditions of employment.

   - Shall provide upon the request of the certificated individual a written statement of specific reason for recommendations that lead to the denial of increments, significant changes in employment, or termination of employment.

   - Shall not assist entry into or continuance in the profession of any person known to be unqualified in accordance with these Principles of Professional Conduct for the Education Profession in Florida and other applicable Florida Statutes and State Board of Education Rules.

   - Shall self-report within forty-eight (48) hours to appropriate authorities (as determined by district) any arrests/charges involving the abuse of a child or the sale and/or possession of a controlled substance. Such notice shall not be considered an admission of guilt nor shall such notice be admissible for any purpose in any proceeding, civil or criminal, administrative or judicial, investigatory or adjudicatory. In addition, shall self-report any conviction, finding of guilt, withholding of adjudication, commitment to a pretrial diversion program, or entering of a plea of guilty or Nolo Contendere for any criminal offense other than a minor traffic violation within forty-eight (48) hours after the final judgment. When handling sealed and expunged records disclosed under this rule, school districts shall comply with the confidentiality provisions of Sections 943.0585(4)(c) and 943.059(4)(c), Florida Statutes.

   - Shall report to appropriate authorities any known allegation of a violation of the Florida School Code or State Board of Education Rules as defined in Section 1012.795(1), Florida Statutes.

Self-reporting issues of abuse or criminal activity within forty-eight hours is mandatory for teachers involved in any arrests/charges involving the abuse of a child or the sale or possession of illegal drugs. Teachers are put on immediate suspension with pay pending the outcome of an investigation. District investigators are sent to school communities to gather data from witnesses, computers, and administrators to provide evidence to either support or refute the pending case.

Teachers can appeal a suspension by sending a letter to the district either personally or from a lawyer representative to appeal the suspension and refute the charges. The school board makes the final decision to revoke or suspend a certificate if the charges are not criminally pending by the police or through the legal system. The superintendent provides the final closure for filing revoked or suspended certificates.

COMPETENCY 7

KNOWLEDGE OF HOW TO APPLY HUMAN DEVELOPMENT AND LEARNING THEORIES THAT SUPPORT THE INTELLECTUAL, PERSONAL, AND SOCIAL DEVELOPMENT OF ALL STUDENTS

SKILL 7.1 Identify patterns of physical, social, and academic development of students

To be successful, a teacher must have a broad knowledge and thorough understanding of the development that typically occurs during the students' current period of life. More important, the teacher understands how children learn best during each period of development. The most important premise of child development is that all domains of development (physical, social, and academic) are integrated. Development in each dimension is influenced by the other dimensions. Moreover, today's educator must also have knowledge of exceptionalities and how these exceptionalities affect all domains of a child's development.

Physical Development

It is important for the teacher to be aware of the physical stage of development and how the child's physical growth and development affect the child's cognitive learning. Factors determined by the physical stage of development include: ability to sit and attend, the need for activity, the relationship between physical skills and self-esteem, and the degree to which physical involvement in an activity (as opposed to being able to understand an abstract concept) affects learning.

Cognitive (Academic) Development

Children go through patterns of learning, beginning with pre-operational thought processes, and they move to concrete operational thoughts. Eventually they begin to acquire the mental ability to think about and solve problems in their head because they can manipulate objects symbolically. Children of most ages can use symbols such as words and numbers to represent objects and relations, but they need concrete reference points. To facilitate cognitive development, it is essential that children be encouraged to use and develop the thinking skills that they possess in solving problems that interest them. The content of the curriculum must be relevant, engaging, and meaningful to the students.

Social Development

Children progress through a variety of social stages. First, they begin with an awareness of their peers but have a lack of concern for the presence of these other children. Young children engage in "parallel" activities playing alongside their peers without directly interacting with one another. Next, during the primary years, children develop an intense interest in peers. They establish productive, positive social and working relationships with one another. This stage of social growth continues throughout the child's formative period including the primary, middle, and high school years. It is necessary for teachers to recognize the importance of developing positive peer-group relationships and to provide opportunities and support for cooperative small group projects that not only develop cognitive ability but also promote peer interaction. The ability to work and relate effectively with peers is of major importance and contributes greatly to the child's sense of competence. In order to develop this sense of competence, children need to be successful in acquiring the knowledge and skills recognized by their culture as important; in the United States, among the most important are those skills that promote academic achievement.

The ability to work and relate effectively with peers is of major importance and contributes greatly to the child's sense of competence.

Developmental Orientation

Knowledge of age-appropriate expectations is fundamental to both the teacher's positive relationship with students and his or her ability to develop effective instructional strategies. Equally important is the knowledge of what is appropriate for individual children in a classroom. DEVELOPMENTALLY ORIENTED TEACHERS approach classroom groups and individual students with a respect for their

DEVELOPMENTALLY ORIENTED TEACHERS: teachers that approach classroom groups and individual students with a respect for their emerging capabilities

emerging capabilities. Developmentalists recognize that kids grow in common patterns but at different rates, which usually cannot be accelerated by adult pressure or input. These teachers also know that variations in the school performance of different children often results from differences in their general growth. Most school districts use inclusion to ensure that all children receive a free and appropriate education. Therefore, it is vital for teachers to know the characteristics of students' exceptionalities and their implications for learning.

SKILL 7.2 **Identify motivational strategies and factors that encourage students to be achievement and goal oriented**

Teachers need to be aware that much of what they say and do can be motivating and may have a positive effect on students' achievement.

Teachers need to be aware that much of what they say and do can be motivating and may have a positive effect on students' achievement. Studies have been conducted to determine the impact of teacher behavior on student performance. Surprisingly, a teacher's voice can make a real impression on students. The human voice has several dimensions, including volume, pitch, rate, etc. A recent study on the effects of speech rate indicates that, although both boys and girls prefer to listen at a rate of about 200 words per minute, boys tend to prefer slower rates than girls. This same study indicates that a slower rate of speech directly affects processing ability and comprehension.

Teachers as Motivators

Other speech factors correlate with teaching-criterion scores including:

- Communication of ideas
- Communication of emotion
- Distinctness/pronunciation
- Quality variation and phrasing

These scores show that "good" teachers ("good" meaning teachers who positively impact and motivate students) use more variety in speech than do less effective teachers. Thus, a teacher's speech skills can be strong motivating elements. Body language has an even greater effect on student achievement and ability to set and focus on goals. Smiles provide support and give feedback about the teacher's affective state—a deadpan expression can actually be detrimental to student progress, and frowns are perceived by students to mean displeasure, disapproval, and even anger. Studies also show that teacher posture and movement are indicators of their enthusiasm and energy, which emphatically influence student outcomes including learning, attitudes, motivation, and focus on goals. Teachers are second only to parents in their effect on student motivation.

Hands-on learning

Teachers can also enhance student motivation by planning and directing interactive, hands-on learning experiences. Research substantiates that cooperative group projects decrease student behavior problems and increase student on-task behavior. Students who are directly involved with learning activities are more motivated to complete a task to the best of their ability.

SKILL 7.3 **Identify activities to accommodate different learning needs, developmental levels, and experiential backgrounds**

Selection of Learning Activities

The effective teacher is cognizant of students' individual learning styles, human growth, and development theories, and how to apply these principles in the selection and implementation of appropriate instructional activities. Learning activities selected for early childhood (below age eight) should occur in short time frames in highly simplified form. The nature of the activity and the context in which the activity is presented affects the approach that the students will take in processing the information. During early childhood, children tend to process information at a slower rate than when they are older (age eight and beyond).

> The effective teacher is cognizant of students' individual learning styles, human growth, and development theories, and how to apply these principles in the selection and implementation of appropriate instructional activities.

Selecting activities

When selecting and implementing learning activities for older children, teachers should focus on more complex instructional activities for which these children are developmentally prepared. Moreover, effective teachers maintain a clear understanding of the developmental appropriateness of activities selected. They also present these activities in a manner consistent with the level of readiness of their students.

Teaching was once seen as a simple job of developing lesson plans, teaching, going home early, and taking the summer off. However, the demands of a classroom involve much more than grading papers. To begin with, the single task of writing lesson plans is very complicated. LESSON PLANS help guide classroom instruction and incorporates the nuts and bolts of a teaching unit. It outlines the steps to both implement the lesson and assess the capacity of the teacher's instruction and the students' learning. Through the lesson plan, teachers identify their objectives and quantify learning goals. They then incorporate effective performance-based assessments to identify when students have learned the material presented.

> **LESSON PLAN:** a plan that outlines the steps to both implement the lesson and assess the capacity of the teacher's instruction and the students' learning

Planning for Classroom Instruction

The effective teacher takes care to select appropriate activities and classroom situations in which learning is optimized. Instructional activities and classroom conditions should be manipulated in a manner that enhances group and individual learning opportunities. For example, the classroom teacher can plan group activities in which students cooperate, share ideas, and discuss topics. In addition to enhancing academic growth, cooperative learning can teach students to collaborate and share personal and cultural ideas and values.

> *The effective teacher takes care to select appropriate activities and classroom situations in which learning is optimized.*

Selecting learning activities

The effective teacher selects learning activities based on specific learning objectives. Ideally, teachers should only plan activities that augment the specific objectives of the lesson and reinforce the teacher's presentation. Additionally, selected learning objectives should be consistent with state and district educational goals, which in turn should focus on national educational goals (Goals 2000). Lesson plans should also target the specific strengths and weaknesses of individual students. The effective teacher plans his/her learning activities to introduce them in a meaningful instructional sequence with relevant activities reinforcing instruction.

SKILL 7.4 Apply knowledge of learning theories to classroom practices

Learning Theories

A classic learning theorist, Piaget believed children passed through a series of stages to develop from the most basic forms of concrete thinking to sophisticated levels of abstract thinking. His developmental theory consists of four learning stages, which can be remembered with the following mnemonic, Stages Precious Children Follow (SPCF):

1. Sensory motor stage: From birth to age two

2. Preoperation stage: Ages two to seven or early elementary

3. Concrete operational: Ages seven to eleven or upper elementary

4. Formal operational: Ages seven to fifteen or late elementary/high school

Additional prominent learning theories in education today include brain-based learning and the Multiple Intelligence Theory. Supported by recent brain research, brain-based learning suggests that knowledge about the way the brain retains information enables educators to design the most effective learning environments. As a result, researchers have developed twelve principles that relate knowledge about the brain to teaching practices.

> ### The twelve principles of brain-based learning:
> - The brain is a complex adaptive system
> - The brain is social
> - The search for meaning is innate
> - We use patterns to learn more effectively
> - Emotions are crucial to developing patterns
> - Each brain perceives and creates parts and whole simultaneously
> - Learning involves focused and peripheral attention
> - Learning involves conscious and unconscious processes
> - We have at least two ways of organizing memory
> - Learning is developmental
> - Complex learning is enhanced by challenge (and inhibited by threat)
> - Every brain is unique
>
> Caine & Caine, 1994, Mind/Brain Learning Principles

To maximize student learning, educators can use these principles to help design methods and environments in their classrooms. The Multiple Intelligence Theory, developed by Howard Gardner, suggests that students learn in at least seven different ways: visually/spatially, musically, verbally, logically/mathematically, interpersonally, intrapersonally, and bodily/kinesthetically.

Today, teachers are immediately faced with the challenge of deciding whether they believe that the classroom should be teacher-centered or student-centered. Usually, an appropriate combination of both is preferred; thus, most teachers must negotiate which areas of their instruction should be teacher-centered and which areas should be student-centered.

Classroom Styles

TEACHER-CENTERED CLASSROOMS generally focus on the concept that knowledge is objective and that students must learn new information through the transmission of that knowledge from the teacher. **STUDENT-CENTERED CLASSROOMS** are considered to be constructivist, in that students are given opportunities to construct their own meanings onto new pieces of knowledge. Doing so may require that students are more actively involved in the learning process. Indeed, constructivism is a strong force in teaching today, but it is often misinterpreted. Good constructivist teachers do NOT just let their students explore anything they want in any way they choose; rather, they give students opportunities to learn things in more natural ways, such as through experiments, hands-on projects, discussions, etc.

TEACHER-CENTERED CLASSROOMS: classrooms that focus on the concept that knowledge is objective and that students must learn new information through the transmission of that knowledge from the teacher

STUDENT-CENTERED CLASSROOMS: classrooms in which students are given opportunities to construct their own meanings onto new pieces of knowledge; these classrooms are considered constructivist

Constructivist theory

The most current theory of constructivist learning allows students to construct learning opportunities. For constructivist teachers, the belief is that students create their own reality of knowledge and how to process and observe the world around them. Students are constantly constructing new ideas, which serve as frameworks for learning and teaching. Researchers have shown that the constructivist model is composed of four components:

CONSTRUCTIVIST LEARNING
Learner creates knowledge
Learner constructs and makes meaningful new knowledge to existing knowledge
Learner shapes and constructs knowledge by life experiences and social interactions
The student, teacher and classmates establish knowledge cooperatively on a daily basis

According to Kelly (1969), "human beings construct knowledge systems based on their observations"; this statement parallels Jean Piaget's theory that knowledge is constructed as individuals work with others who have similar background and thought processes. Constructivist learning for students is dynamic and ongoing. For constructivist teachers, the classroom becomes a place where students are supported and encouraged to interact with the instructional process by asking questions and applying new ideas to old theories.

Cognitive theory

Researchers Joyce and Weil (1996) described THE THEORY OF METACOGNITION as first the study of how to help the learner gain understanding about how knowledge is constructed; and second, arming that learner with the conscious tools for constructing that knowledge. The COGNITIVE APPROACH to learning emphasizes that the teacher must understand that the greatest learning and retention opportunities in the classroom come from teaching the student to process his or her own learning to master the skill being taught. Students are taught to develop concepts and teach themselves skills in problem solving and critical thinking. The student becomes the active participant in the learning process and the teacher becomes the facilitator of that conceptual and cognitive learning process.

Social and behavioral theories

Social and behavioral theories look at how students' social interactions instruct or impact learning opportunities in the classroom. Both theories are

THE THEORY OF META-COGNITION: the study of how to help the learner gain understanding about how knowledge is constructed and arming that learner with the conscious tools for constructing that knowledge

COGNITIVE APPROACH: students are taught to develop concepts and teach themselves skills in problem solving and critical thinking

subject to individual variables that are learned and applied either positively or negatively in the classroom. Innumerable stimuli in the classroom can promote learning or evoke behavior that is counterproductive for both students and teachers. As human beings, students are social and normally gravitate to action in the classroom; to maximize learning opportunities, teachers must be deliberate in planning classroom environments that provide both focus and engagement.

Designing a classroom

Designing classrooms that provide optimal academic and behavioral support for diverse students can be daunting. The ultimate goal is creating a safe learning environment where students can construct knowledge in an engaging and positive climate.

No one of these theories will work for every classroom and a good approach is to incorporate a range of learning theories. Still, under the guidance of any theory, good educators will differentiate their instructional practices to meet the needs of individual students' abilities and interests using various instructional practices.

SKILL 7.5 Identify characteristics of, and intervention strategies for, students with disabilities

Many types of disabilities are found in children and adults. Some are entirely physical, while others are entirely related to learning and the mind. Some involve a combination of both. When a teacher notices abnormalities in the classroom, such as a student's incredible ability to solve a math problem without working it out (a potential attribute of giftedness) or another student's extreme trouble with spelling (a potential attribute of dyslexia), he may suspect a disability is present.

Common learning disabilities include:

- Attention deficit hyperactivity disorder: Impaired concentration
- Auditory processing disorders: Impaired listening comprehension
- Visual processing disorders: Impaired reading and/or visual memory
- Dyslexia: Impaired reading ability

Some physical disabilities include:

- Down's Syndrome
- Cerebral Palsy

Developmental disabilities might include the lack of ability to use fine motor skills.

When giftedness is observed, teachers should also concern themselves with ensuring that such children receive the attention they need and deserve so they can continue to learn and grow.

The list of possible disabilities is almost endless. When a teacher notices a potential disability, he or she might seek the help of specialists within the school to determine if further testing or intervention is needed.

Student-Centered Classrooms

A teacher's responsibility to students extends beyond the four walls of the school building. In addition to offering well-planned and articulately delivered lessons, the teacher must consider the effects of both body language and spoken language on students' learning. Furthermore, today's educator must address the needs of diverse learners within a single classroom. The teacher is able to attain materials that may be necessary for the majority of the regular education students, some of the special needs children, and, more and more frequently, an individual student. The effective teacher knows that there are hundreds of adaptive materials that could be used to help these students increase achievement and develop skills.

Today's educator must address the needs of diverse learners within a single classroom.

Student-centered classrooms not only contain textbooks, workbooks, and literature materials, but also rely heavily on a variety of audio-visual equipment and computers. There are tape recorders, language masters, and DVD players to help meet the learning styles of some of the students.

Although most school centers cannot supply all of the possible materials that all special needs students within their school may require, each district likely has a resource center where teachers can borrow special equipment. Most community support agencies offer assistance in providing necessary equipment or materials to serve students and adults with special needs. Teachers must be familiar with procedures to obtain a wide range of materials, including:

- School supplies
- Medical care
- Clothing
- Food
- Adaptive
- Computers

- Books with large print or Braille
- Eyeglasses
- Hearing aids
- Wheelchairs
- Counseling
- Transportation

Many special needs students have an Individual Educational Plan (IEP) or a 504 plan. These documents clearly state the students' educational objectives and learning needs, as well as the people responsible for meeting these objectives.

A well-written IEP will contain evidence that the student is receiving resources from the school and discuss the community that will assist in helping to meet the physical, social, and academic needs of the student.

The challenges of meeting the needs of all students in the classroom require that the teacher himself be a lifelong learner. Ongoing participation in professional staff development; attendance at local, state, and national conferences; and continuing education classes help teachers grow professionally.

Individuals with Disabilities Education Act and Child Study Teams

Collaborative teams play a crucial role in meeting the needs of all students, and they are important in identifying students with special needs. Under the INDIVIDUALS WITH DISABILITIES EDUCATION ACT (IDEA), it is the responsibility of public schools to ensure consultative, evaluative, and, if necessary, prescriptive services to children with special needs.

In most school districts, this responsibility is handled by a collaborative group called the CHILD STUDY TEAM (CST). If a teacher or parent suspects a child to have academic, social, or emotional problems the child is referred to the CST where a team consisting of educational professionals (including teachers, specialists, the school psychologist, guidance, and other support staff) review the student's case and situation through meetings with the teacher and/or parents/guardians. The CST will determine what evaluations or tests are necessary. They will also assess the results and suggest a plan of action if one is necessary.

Inclusion, mainstreaming, and least restrictive environment

Inclusion, mainstreaming, and least restrictive environment are interrelated policies under the IDEA, with varying degrees of statutory imperatives.

- Inclusion: The right of students with disabilities to be placed in the regular classroom

- Lease restrictive environment: The mandate that children be educated to the maximum extent appropriate with their nondisabled peers

- Mainstreaming: A policy whereby disabled students can be placed in the regular classroom, as long as such placement does not interfere with the student's educational plan

> A teacher's job would be relatively easy if simply instructing students in current curriculum objectives was his or her only responsibility. Today's educator must first ensure that the students are able to come to school, are able to attend to the curriculum, have their individual learning styles met, and are motivated to work to their fullest capacity.

INDIVIDUALS WITH DISABILITIES EDUCATION ACT (IDEA): the federal act that mandates special education services in every state

CHILD STUDY TEAM (CST): a collaborative group that ensures consultative, evaluative, and, if necessary, prescriptive services to children with special needs

ACADEMIC INTERVENTION PLAN (AIP): consists of additional instructional services that are provided to the student in order to help him or her better meet academic goals

504 PLAN: a plan of instructional services to assist students with special needs in a regular education classroom setting

INDIVIDUALIZED EDUCATION PLAN (IEP): a legal document that delineates the specific adapted services a student with disabilities will receive

One plan of action is an ACADEMIC INTERVENTION PLAN (AIP). An AIP consists of additional instructional services that are provided to the student in order to help her better meet academic goals. Often these plans are developed if the student has met certain criteria (such as scoring below the state reference point on standardized tests or performing more than two levels below grade level).

Another plan of action is a 504 plan. A 504 PLAN is a legal document based on the provisions of the Rehabilitation Act of 1973 (which preceded IDEA). A 504 plan is a plan of instructional services to assist students with special needs in a regular education classroom setting. When a student's physical, emotional, or other impairments impact his ability to learn in a regular education classroom setting, that student can be referred for a 504 meeting. Typically, the CST and perhaps even the student's physician or therapist will participate in the 504 meeting and review the student's specific needs to determine if a 504 plan will be written.

Finally, a child referred to CST may qualify for an INDIVIDUALIZED EDUCATION PLAN (IEP). An IEP is a legal document that delineates the specific adapted services a student with disabilities will receive. An IEP differs from a 504 plan in that the child must be identified for special education services to qualify for an IEP, and all students who receive special education services must have an IEP. Each IEP must contain statements pertaining to the student's:

- Present performance level
- Annual goals
- Related services
- Supplementary aids
- Testing modifications
- Projected date of services
- Assessment methods for monitoring progress

At least once each year, the CST and guardians must meet to review and update a student's IEP.

Special education teachers, resource specialists, school psychologists, and other special education staff are present on school campuses to be resources for students who have special educational needs. Occasionally, new teachers fear that when a resource specialist seeks to work with them, it means that the resource specialist does not think the teacher is doing an adequate job in dealing with students with IEPs. Quite the contrary is true. Many IEPs require that resource specialists work in students' general education classrooms. Considering that school is about more than just the learning of content standards—rather, it is often about socialization and the development of citizens for a democratic society—it is both counterproductive and unfair to exclude students from regular classrooms, even if they need some individualized assistance from a special education resource teacher.

First and foremost, teachers must be familiar with what is stated in their students' IEPs. For example, some IEPs have explicit strategies that teachers should use to help the students learn effectively.

Additionally, teachers may want to provide additional attention to these students to ensure that they are progressing effectively. Sometimes, it may be necessary to reduce or modify assignments for students with disabilities. For example, if a teacher were to assign fifteen math problems for homework, the assignment might be more effective for the students with disabilities if it is only five problems. Teachers can use multiple strategies, group students in flexible situations, and pair them with others who can be of greater assistance.

Finally, welcome and include the suggestions and assistance of the special education staff. Most resource specialists are trained specifically to work with general education teachers, and most want to be able to do that in the most effective, nonthreatening way.

Creating the Least Restrictive Environment

Special education services are offered in many ways, and a student's IEP will determine what services are appropriate and how to deliver them in the least restrictive environment. Inclusion refers to the situation where a student with special needs remains in the regular education classroom with the support of special education support staff (sometimes in the form of a personal or class aid). Sometimes a student requires some resource room, or pull out, services. In these cases, students are taken into smaller class settings where personalized services are delivered in their greatest area(s) of difficulty. Students who have difficulty functioning in a regular education classroom are placed in smaller classrooms for the full school day. These are sometimes referred to as learning disabled, or LD, classrooms.

Per federal law, students with disabilities should be included as much as possible in the general education curriculum of their schools. While this may be difficult for new teachers (likewise, it may be difficult for new teachers to include gifted students in the general education curriculum), it is extremely important to do so.

Flexible grouping is a unique strategy to ensure that students with special needs are fully accommodated. Although flexible grouping can involve groups that will change (depending on the activity, or just depending on the need to rotate groups), when teachers consistently build in various group structures in order to accommodate different learning needs, their students will get varied and numerous opportunities to talk about, reflect upon, and question new learning. In some cases, teachers may wish to pair students with special needs with other students who are proficient in particular subjects; at other times, they may desire to pair students with others who have similar levels of proficiency.

Behavior issues often cause students with special needs to be excluded from full class participation. It is important for teachers to note that often, students with special needs do not want to be excluded, and often, they do not want to be "bad." Rather, they are seeking attention, or they are bored. In either case, classroom activities must be developed with these concerns in mind. All students, in fact, will be more engaged with hands-on, real-world learning activities. Often, when teachers give students even small amounts of choice, such as letting them choose one of three topics to write about, students feel empowered. Students with special needs are no different.

Often, when teachers give students even small amounts of choice, such as letting them choose one of three topics to write about, students feel empowered. Students with special needs are no different.

Finally, many students with special needs want to stay "caught up" with the rest of the class, but occasionally, they cannot. In such cases, it is imperative that teachers find ways to show these students that they are on the same page as the rest of the class. Reducing the amount of work for students with special needs is often productive; pairing such students with more proficient students can also be assistive.

Students with exceptional abilities can also be a challenge for teachers. It is unfair to assume that because these students already "get it," they can be ignored. These students need to continue to learn, even if it is above and beyond the rest of the class. Furthermore, they will often resent being smarter than the rest of the class because they are called on more or treated as if they do not need any attention. While these students are a fantastic resource for the rest of the class, being a resource is not their role in the classroom. They are there to learn, just like the rest of the class. They do not simply need more work; rather, they occasionally need different work to engage them and stimulate their minds.

COMPETENCY 8
KNOWLEDGE OF EFFECTIVE READING STRATEGIES THAT CAN BE APPLIED ACROSS THE CURRICULUM TO INCREASE LEARNING

SKILL Identify effective instructional methods to develop text reading
8.1 skills *(i.e., phonemic awareness, phonics, and fluency)*

In 2000, the National Reading Panel released its now well-known report on teaching children to read. This report partially put to rest the debate between phonics and whole language. It essentially argued that word–letter recognition is as important as understanding what the text means. The report's "Big 5" critical areas of reading instruction are explained in the following sections.

Phonemic Awareness

PHONEMIC AWARENESS is the acknowledgement of sounds and words; for example, a child's realization that some words rhyme is one of the skills that fall under this category. *Onset* and *rhyme* are skills that might help students learn that the sound of the first letter "b" in the word "bad" can be changed with the sound "d" to make it "dad." The key in phonemic awareness is that it can be taught with the students' eyes closed; in other words, it's all about understanding sounds, not ascribing written letters to sounds.

> **PHONEMIC AWARENESS:** the acknowledgement of sounds and words

Phonics

As opposed to phonemic awareness, the study of phonics must be done with the eyes open. PHONICS is the connection between sounds and the letters on a page. In other words, students learning phonics might see the word "bad" and sound each letter out slowly until they recognize that they just said the word.

> **PHONICS:** the connection between sounds and the letters on a page

Fluency

When students practice FLUENCY, they practice reading connected pieces of text. In other words, instead of looking at a word as just a word, they might read a sentence straight through. The point of fluency is for the student to comprehend what he or she is reading by putting words in a sentence together quickly. If a student is NOT fluent in reading, he or she would sound each letter or word out

> **FLUENCY:** reading connected pieces of text

slowly and pay more attention to the phonics of each word. A fluent reader, on the other hand, might read a sentence out loud using appropriate intonations.

The best way to test for fluency is to have a student read something out loud, preferably a few sentences in a row. Most students just learning to read will not be very fluent right away, but with practice, they will increase their fluency. Even though fluency is not the same as comprehension, fluency is a good predictor of comprehension; when the student is freed from focusing on sounding out each word, he or she can shift attention to the meaning of the words.

Comprehension

COMPREHENSION:
when the reader can
ascribe meaning to text

COMPREHENSION simply means that the reader can ascribe meaning to text. Even though students may be good with phonics, and may know what many words on a page mean, some of them are not able to demonstrate comprehension because they do not have the tools to help them comprehend. For example, students should know that stories often have structures (beginning, middle, and end). They should also know that when they are reading something and it does not make sense, they will need to employ "fix-up" strategies where they go back into the text they just read and look for clues. Teachers can use many strategies to teach comprehension, including questioning, asking students to paraphrase or summarize, utilizing graphic organizers, and focusing on mental images.

Vocabulary

Students will be better at comprehension if they have a stronger working vocabulary. Research has shown that students learn more vocabulary when it is presented in context, rather than in vocabulary lists, for example. Furthermore, the more students get to use particular words in context, the more they will remember each word and utilize the words in the comprehension of sentences that contain the words.

Methods used to teach these skills are often featured in a balanced literacy curriculum, which focuses on the use of skills in various instructional contexts. For example, with independent reading, students independently choose books that are at their reading levels; with guided reading, teachers work with small groups of students to help them with their particular reading problems; with whole group reading, the entire class will read the same text, and the teacher will incorporate activities to help students learn phonics, comprehension, fluency, and vocabulary. In addition to these components of balanced literacy, teachers incorporate writing so that students can learn the structures of communicating through text.

While teachers can anticipate that certain skills can be mastered by certain ages, all children are different. When development is too far off the general target, intervention may be necessary.

By their first year, babies can identify words and notice the social and directive impacts of language. By their second year, children have decent vocabularies, they make-believe that they are reading books (especially if their role models read), and they can follow simple oral stories. By their third year, children have more advanced skills in listening and speaking. Within the next few years, children are capable of using longer sentences, retelling parts of stories, counting, and "scribbling" messages. They are capable of learning the basics of phonemic awareness.

At about five years old, children are really ready to begin learning phonics. Many teachers mistake phonics as being just a step in the process toward comprehension, when in fact, children are fully capable of learning how to comprehend and make meaning at the same age. Phonics, though, will ideally be mastered by second to third grade.

For more information on the stages of language acquisition, see:

http://www.learningpt.org/ pdfs/literacy/readingbirth-tofive.pdf

SKILL 8.2 Identify instructional methods and strategies for developing and using content area vocabulary

CONTENT AREA VOCABULARY is the specific vocabulary related to particular concepts of various academic disciplines (social science, science, math, art, etc).

CONTENT AREA VO-CABULARY: the specific vocabulary related to particular concepts of various academic disciplines (social science, science, math, art, etc.)

While teachers tend to think of content area vocabulary as something that should be focused on just at the secondary level (middle and high school), even elementary school students studying various subjects will understand concepts better when the vocabulary used to describe them is explicitly explained. But it is true that in the secondary level, where students go to different teachers for each subject, content area vocabulary becomes more emphasized.

Often, educators believe that vocabulary should just be taught in a language arts class, not realizing that there is not enough time for students to learn the enormous vocabulary in only one class in order to be successful with a standards-based education and that the teaching of vocabulary related to a particular subject is a very good way to help students understand the subject better.

First and foremost, teachers should teach strategies to determine the meanings for difficult vocabulary when students encounter it on their own. Teachers can do this by teaching students how to identify the meanings of words in context (usually through activities where the word is taken out, and the students have to figure out a way to make sense of the sentence). In addition, dictionary skills must be taught in all subject areas. Teachers should also consider that teaching vocabulary is not just the teaching of words; rather, it is the teaching of complex concepts, each with histories and connotations.

When teachers explicitly teach vocabulary, it is best if they can connect new words to ideas, words, and experiences with which students are already familiar. This will help to reduce the strangeness of the new words. Furthermore, the more concrete the examples, the more likely students will be able to use the word in context.

Finally, students need plenty of exposure to the new words. They need to be able to hear and use the new words in many naturally produced sentences. The more one hears and uses a sentence in context, the more the word is solidified in the person's long-term vocabulary.

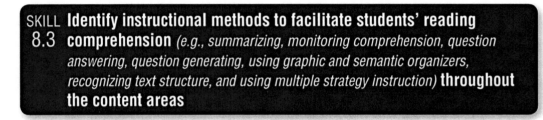

SKILL 8.3 **Identify instructional methods to facilitate students' reading comprehension** *(e.g., summarizing, monitoring comprehension, question answering, question generating, using graphic and semantic organizers, recognizing text structure, and using multiple strategy instruction)* **throughout the content areas**

The point of comprehension instruction is not necessarily to focus just on the text(s) students are using at the very moment of instruction, but rather to help them learn the strategies that they can use independently with any other text.

COMMON METHODS OF TEACHING INSTRUCTION	
Summarization	Students go over the main point of the text, along with strategically chosen details that highlight the main point. This is not the same as paraphrasing, which is saying the same thing in different words. Teaching students how to summarize is very important because it will help them look for the most critical areas in a text and in nonfiction. For example, it will help them distinguish between main arguments and examples. In fiction, it helps students to learn how to focus on the main characters and events and distinguish those from the lesser characters and events.
Question Answering	While this tends to be overused in many classrooms, it is still a valid method of teaching students to comprehend. Students answer questions regarding a text, either out loud, in small groups, or individually on paper. The best questions are those that cause students to think about the text (rather than just find an answer within the text).
Question Generating	This is the opposite of question answering, although students can then be asked to answer their own questions or the questions of peers. In general, we want students to constantly question texts as they read. This is important because it causes students to become more critical readers. To teach students to generate questions helps them to learn the types of questions they can ask and it gets them thinking about how best to be critical of texts.

Continued on next page

Graphic Organizers	Graphic organizers are graphical representations of content within a text. For example, Venn diagrams can be used to highlight the difference between two characters in a novel or two similar political concepts in a social studies textbook. Or, a teacher can use flow-charts with students to talk about the steps in a process, such as the steps of setting up a science experiment or the chronological events of a story. Semantic organizers are similar in that they graphically display information. The difference, usually, is that semantic organizers focus on words or concepts. For example, a word web can help students make sense of a word by mapping out from the central word all the similar and related concepts to that word.
Text Structure	Often in nonfiction—particularly in textbooks—and sometimes in fiction, text structures will give important clues to readers about what to look for. Students may not know how to make sense of all the types of headings in a textbook and do not realize that, for example, the side-bar story about a character in history is not the main text on a particular page in the history textbook. Teaching students how to interpret text structures gives them tools with which to tackle similar texts.
Monitoring Comprehension	Students need to be aware of their comprehension, or lack of it, in particular texts. So, it is important to teach students what to do when suddenly text stops making sense. For example, students can go back and reread the description of a character. Or, they can go back to the table of contents or the first paragraph of a chapter to see where they are headed.
Textual Marking	This is where students interact with the text as they read. For example, armed with sticky notes, students can insert questions or comments regarding specific sentences or paragraphs within the text. This helps students focus on the importance of the small things, particularly when they are reading larger works (such as novels in high school). It also gives students a reference point on which to go back into the text when they need to review something.
Discussion	Small group or whole-class discussion stimulates thoughts about texts and gives students a larger picture of the impact of those texts. For example, teachers can strategically encourage students to discuss related concepts to the text. This helps students learn to consider texts within larger societal and social concepts. Or teachers can encourage students to provide personal opinions in discussion. By listening to various students' opinions, this will help all students in a class to see the wide range of possible interpretations and thoughts regarding one text.

Many people mistakenly believe that the terms "research-based," "research-validated," or "evidence-based" relate mainly to specific programs, such as early reading textbook programs. While research does validate that some of these programs are effective, much research has been conducted regarding the effectiveness of particular instructional strategies. In reading, many of these strategies have been documented in the report from the National Reading Panel (2000).

Just because a strategy has not been validated as effective by research, however, does not necessarily mean that it is not effective with certain students in certain situations. The number of strategies out there far outweighs researchers' ability to test their effectiveness. Some of the strategies listed above have been validated by rigorous research, while others have been shown consistently to help improve students' reading abilities in localized situations. There simply is not enough space to list all the strategies out there that have been proven effective; just know that the above strategies are very commonly cited as working in a variety of situations.

SKILL 8.4 Identify strategies for developing critical thinking skills (e.g., analysis, synthesis, evaluation)

Developing critical thinking skills in students is not as simple as developing other simpler skills. In fact, many teachers mistakenly believe that these skills can be taught out of context (i.e., they can be taught as skills in and of themselves). Good teachers, however, realize that critical thinking skills must be taught within the contexts of specific subject matter. For example, language arts teachers can teach critical thinking skills through novels; social studies teachers can teach critical thinking skills through primary source documents or current events; science teachers can teach critical thinking skills by having students develop hypotheses prior to conducting experiments.

First, let's start with definitions of the various types of critical thinking skills. ANALYSIS is the systematic exploration of a concept, event, term, piece of writing, element of media, or any other complex item. Usually, people think of analysis as the exploration of the parts that make up a whole. For example, when someone analyzes a piece of literature, that person might focus on small pieces of the literature; yet, as they focus on the small pieces, they also call attention to the big picture and show how the small pieces create significance for the whole novel.

> **ANALYSIS:** the systematic exploration of a concept, event, term, piece of writing, element of media, or any other complex item

To carry this example further, if one were to analyze a novel, that person might investigate a particular character to determine how that character adds significance to the whole novel. In something more concrete like biology, one could analyze the findings of an experiment to see if the results might indicate significance for something even larger than the experiment itself. It is very easy to analyze political events, for example. A social studies teacher could ask students to analyze the events leading up to World War II; doing so would require that students look at the small pieces (i.e., smaller world events prior to World War II) and determine how those small pieces, when added up together, caused the war.

> **SYNTHESIS:** taking different things and making them one whole thing

Next, let's consider synthesis. SYNTHESIS is usually thought of to be the opposite of analysis. In analysis, we take a whole, break it up into pieces, and look at the pieces. With synthesis, we take different things and make them one whole thing. For example, a language arts teacher could ask students to synthesize two works of distinct literature. Let's say that we take *The Scarlet Letter* and *The Crucible*, two works both featuring life during Puritan America, written about one century apart. A student could synthesize the two works and come to conclusions about

Puritan life. An art teacher could ask students to synthesize two paintings from the Impressionist era and come to conclusions about the features that distinguish that style of art.

Finally, EVALUATION involves making judgments. Whereas analysis and synthesis seek answers and hypotheses based on investigations, evaluation seeks opinions. For example, a social studies teacher could ask students to evaluate the quality of Richard Nixon's resignation speech. To do so, they would judge whether or not they felt it was good. In contrast, analysis would keep judgment out of the assignment: it would have students focus possibly on the structure of the speech (i.e., Does an argument move from emotional to logical?). When evaluating a speech, a piece of literature, a movie, or a work of art, we seek to determine whether one thinks it is good or not. But keep in mind that teaching good evaluation skills requires not just that students learn how to determine whether something is good or not—it requires that they learn how to support their evaluations. So, if a student claims that Nixon's speech was effective in what the President intended the speech to do, the student would need to explain how this is so. Notice that evaluation will probably utilize the skills of analysis and/or synthesis, but that the purpose is ultimately different.

> **EVALUATION:**
> making judgments; seeking opinions

In general, critical thinking skills should be taught through assignments, activities, lessons, and discussions that cause students to think on their own. While teachers can and should provide students with the tools to think critically, they will ultimately become critical thinkers if they have to use those tools themselves.

However, this last point cannot be taken lightly: Teachers must provide students with the tools to evaluate, analyze, and synthesize. Let's take political speeches as an example. Students will be better analyzers, synthesizers, and evaluators if they understand some of the basics of political speeches. Therefore, a teacher might introduce concepts such as rhetoric, style, persona, audience, diction, imagery, and tone. The best way to introduce these concepts would be to provide students with multiple good examples of these things. Once they are familiar with these critical tools, students will be in a better place to apply them individually to political speeches—and then be able to analyze, synthesize, and evaluate political speeches on their own.

SKILL 8.5 Identify appropriate references, materials, and technologies for the subject and the students' abilities

Over the last few decades, research has confirmed that students do not all learn in the same way. Furthermore, it has been found that a steady routine of lecture and textbook reading is an extremely ineffective method of instruction. While students definitely should be exposed to lecture and textbooks, they will greatly benefit from the creativity and ingenuity of teachers who find outside resources to assist in the presentation of new knowledge.

Some possibilities outside of the realm of lecture include textual and media references, hands-on materials, and technology. The multiple texts strategy can be used to help students synthesize information and to encourage critical thinking. For example, a social studies teacher might ask students to read an historical novel to complement a unit of study.

In addition to texts, appropriately selected video or audio recordings may be useful. For example, a science teacher may wish to show a short clip of a video that demonstrates how to conduct a particular experiment before students complete the experiment on their own. A language arts teacher may bring in an audio recording of a book to present a uniquely dramatized reading of the book.

Hands-on materials are very important to student learning. For example, math teachers may introduce geometric principles with quilt blocks. Hands-on materials are particularly useful in science subjects; the very idea of a science experiment is that hands-on materials and activities more quickly convey scientific ideas to students than do lectures and textbooks.

Finally, technologies, such as personal computers, are very important for student learning. First, it is extremely important that students learn new technologies so that they are able to easily adapt to the myriad of uses found in business and industry. Second, technology can provide knowledge resources that go beyond what a school library, for example, may be able to offer. Students will need to learn how to search for, evaluate, and utilize appropriate information on the Internet.

SKILL 8.6 Identify methods for differentiating instruction based on student reading data

DIFFERENTIATION OF INSTRUCTION occurs when the teacher will vary the content, process, or product used in instruction (Tomlinson, 1995).

There are three primary ways to differentiate:

- **Content:** The specifics of what is learned. This does not mean that whole units or concepts should be modified. However, within certain topics, specifics can be modified.

- **Process:** The route to learning the content. All students do not have to learn the content using exactly the same method.

- **Product:** The result of the learning. Usually, a product is the result or assessment of learning. For example, not all students are going to demonstrate complete learning on a quiz; likewise, not all students will demonstrate complete learning on a written paper.

There are two keys to successful differentiation:

- **Knowing what is essential in the curriculum:** Although certain things can be modified, other things must remain intact and in a specific order. Disrupting central components of a curriculum can actually damage a student's ability to learn something successfully.

- **Knowing the needs of the students:** While this can take quite some time to figure out, it is very important that teachers pay attention to the interests, tendencies, and abilities of their students so that they understand how each of their students will best learn.

> **DIFFERENTIATION OF INSTRUCTION:** when the teacher varies the content, process, or product used in instruction

Many students will need certain concepts explained in greater depth; others may pick up on concepts rather quickly. For this reason, teachers will want to adapt the curriculum in a way that gives students the opportunity to learn at their own pace while also keeping the class together as a community. Although this can be difficult, the more creative a teacher is with the ways in which students can demonstrate mastery, the more fun the experience will be for students and teachers. Furthermore, teachers will reach students more successfully if they tailor lesson plans, activities, groupings, and other elements of curriculum to each student's need. The reasons for differentiating instruction are based on two important differences in children: interest and ability.

Differentiating Reading Instruction

Differentiating reading instruction is a bit complex. When a teacher wants to ensure that each student in his class is getting the most out of the reading instruction, the teacher will need to consider the level at which the student is proficient in reading—as well as the specific areas in which each student struggles. It is first important to use a variety of sources of data to make decisions on differentiation, rather than rely on just one test, for example.

When teachers have proficient readers in their classrooms, they usually feel that these students need less attention and less work. This is a mistake. If these students are not provided appropriate instruction and challenging activities to increase their reading abilities further, they may become disengaged with school. These students benefit greatly from integrating classroom reading with other types of reading, perhaps complementing the whole-class novel with some additional short stories or nonfiction pieces.

They also benefit from sustained silent reading, in which they can choose their own books and read independently. Discussion groups and teacher-led discussion activities are also very useful for these students. It is important, however, to ensure that these students do not feel that they have to do more work than everyone else. Remember, differentiation does not distinguish differences in quantity; it distinguishes differences in types of work.

Average readers may benefit from many of the things that highly proficient readers do; however, they may need more skill instruction. Most likely, they will not need as much skill instruction as weak readers, but they will benefit highly from having a teacher who knows which skills they are lacking and teaches them to use those skills in their own reading.

Weak readers need to focus highly on skills. Teachers will want to encourage them to make predictions, connect ideas, outline concepts, evaluate, and summarize. The activities that these students engage in should be developed to instill reading strategies that they can use in their independent reading and to propel them toward higher levels of reading.

COMPETENCY 9

KNOWLEDGE OF STRATEGIES TO CREATE AND SUSTAIN A SAFE, EFFICIENT, SUPPORTIVE LEARNING ENVIRONMENT

SKILL 9.1 Evaluate the appropriateness of the physical environment for facilitating student learning and promoting safety

The physical setting of the classroom contributes a great deal toward the propensity for students to learn. An adequate, well-built, and well-equipped classroom will invite students to learn. This has been called invitational learning. Among the important factors to consider in the physical setting of the classroom are:

- Adequate physical space

- Repair status

- Lighting adequacy

- Adequate entry/exit access (including handicap accessibility)

- Ventilation/climate control

- Coloration

A classroom must have adequate physical space so students can conduct themselves comfortably. Some students are distracted by windows, pencil sharpeners, doors, etc. Some students prefer the front, middle, or back rows.

The teacher is responsible for reporting any items of classroom disrepair to maintenance staff. Broken windows, falling plaster, exposed sharp surfaces, leaks in ceiling or walls, and other items of disrepair present hazards to students.

Another factor that must be considered is adequate lighting. Report any inadequacies in classroom illumination. Florescent lights placed at acute angles often burn out faster. A healthy supply of spare tubes is a sound investment.

Local fire and safety codes dictate entry and exit standards. In addition, all corridors and classrooms should be wheelchair accessible for students and others who use them. Older schools may not have this accessibility.

Another consideration is adequate ventilation and climate control. Some classrooms in some states use air conditioning extensively. Sometimes it is so cold as to be considered a distraction. Specialty classes such as science require specialized hoods for ventilation. Physical education classes have the added responsibility for shower areas and specialized environments that must be heated such as pool or athletic training rooms.

Classrooms with warmer, subdued colors contribute to students' concentration on task items. Neutral hues for coloration of walls, ceiling, and carpet or tile are generally used in classrooms to minimize distraction.

In the modern classroom, there is a great deal of furniture, equipment, supplies, appliances, and learning aids to help the teacher teach and students learn. The classroom should be provided with furnishings that fit the purpose of the classroom. The kindergarten classroom may have a reading center, a playhouse, a puzzle table, student work desks/tables, a sandbox, and any other relevant learning/interest areas.

Whatever the arrangement of furniture and equipment may be, the teacher must provide for adequate traffic flow. Rows of desks must have adequate space between them for students to move and for the teacher to circulate. All areas must be open to line-of-sight supervision by the teacher.

Safety in the Classroom

In all cases, proper care must be taken to ensure student safety. Furniture and equipment should be situated safely at all times. No equipment, materials, boxes, and so on should be placed where there is danger of them falling. Doors must have entry and exit accessibility at all times.

The major emergency responses include two categories for student movement: tornado warning response and building evacuation. (Building evacuation includes most other emergencies, such as a fire or bomb threat.)

For tornadoes, the prescribed response is to evacuate all students and personnel to the first floor of multistory buildings and place students along walls away from windows. All persons, including the teacher, should then crouch on the floor and cover their heads with their hands. These are standard procedures for severe weather, particularly tornadoes.

Most other emergency situations require evacuation of the school building. Teachers should be thoroughly familiar with evacuation routes established for each classroom in which they teach. Teachers should accompany and supervise students throughout the evacuation procedure and check to see that all students under their supervision are accounted for. Teachers should then continue to supervise students until the building may be reoccupied (upon proper school or community authority), or until other procedures are followed for students to officially leave the school area and cease to be the supervisory responsibility of the school. Elementary students evacuated to another school can wear nametags and parents or guardians should sign them out at a central location.

SKILL 9.2 **Identify a repertoire of techniques for establishing smooth, efficient, and well-paced routines**

Effective teachers use class time efficiently. This results in higher student subject engagement and will likely result in more subject matter retention.

Punctuality is a part of management of the classroom time. Punctuality can be defined within a classroom setting as beginning class work and activities promptly.

Punctuality is important: if a class is delayed for ten minutes daily over the school year almost two months of instructional time is lost. Therefore, it is very important to be cognizant of making the most of instructional time.

One way teachers use class time efficiently is through a smooth transition from one activity to another; this is also known as management transition. One factor that contributes to efficient management transition is the teacher's management of instructional material. Effective teachers gather their materials during the planning stage of instruction. Doing this, a teacher avoids flipping through things and looking for the items necessary for the current lesson. Momentum is lost and student concentration is broken when this occurs.

> *One way teachers use class time efficiently is through a smooth transition from one activity to another; this is also known as management transition.*

Additionally, teachers who keep students informed of the sequencing of instructional activities maintain systematic transitions because the students are prepared to move on to the next activity. For example, the teacher says, "When we finish with this guided practice together, we will turn to page twenty-three and each student will do the exercises. I will then circulate throughout the classroom helping on an individual basis. Okay, let's begin." Following an example such as this will lead to systematic, smooth transitions between activities because the students will be turning to page twenty-three when the class finishes the practice without a break in concentration.

Another method that leads to smooth transitions is to move students in groups and clusters rather than one by one. This is called group fragmentation. For example, if some students do seat work while other students gather for a reading group, the teacher moves the students in predetermined groups. Instead of calling the individual names of the reading group, which would be time-consuming and laborious, the teacher simply says, "Will the blue reading group please assemble at the reading station? The red and yellow groups will quietly do the vocabulary assignment I am now passing out." As a result of this activity, the classroom is ready to move on in a matter of seconds rather than minutes.

Additionally, the teacher may employ academic transition signals, defined as "teacher utterance[s] that indicate movement of the lesson from one topic or activity to another by indicating where the lesson is and where it is going." For example, the teacher may say, "That completes our description of clouds; now we will examine weather fronts." Like the sequencing of instructional materials, this keeps the student informed on what is coming next so that the students will move to the next activity with little or no break in concentration.

Therefore, effective teachers manage transitions from one activity to another in a systematically oriented way through efficient management of instructional matter, sequencing of instructional activities, moving students in groups, and employing academic transition signals. Through an efficient use of class time, achievement is increased because students spend more class time engaged in on-task behavior.

SKILL 9.3 Identify strategies to involve students in establishing rules and standards for behavior

Teaching social skills can be rather difficult because social competence requires a repertoire of skills in a number of areas. The socially competent person must be able to get along with family and friends, function in a work environment, take care of personal needs, solve problems in daily living, and identify sources of help. A class of students with emotional disabilities may present several deficits in a few areas or a few deficits in many areas. Therefore, the teacher must begin with an assessment of the skill deficits and prioritize the ones to teach first.

TYPE OF ASSESSMENT	DESCRIPTION
Direct Observation	Teacher observes student in various settings with a checklist
Role Play	Teacher observes students in structured scenarios
Teacher Ratings	Teacher rates student with a checklist or formal assessment instrument
Sociometric Measures	*Peer Nomination:* Student names specific classmates who meet a stated criterion (i.e., playmate); score is the number of times a child is nominated *Peer Rating:* Students rank all their classmates on a Likert-type scale (e.g., 1–3 or 1–5 scale) on stated criterion; individual score is the average of the total ratings of their classmates *Paired Comparison:* Student is presented with paired classmate combinations and asked to choose who is most or least liked in the pair

Continued on next page

Context Observation	Student is observed to determine if the skill deficit is present in one setting, but not others
Comparison with Other Student	Student's social skill behavior is compared to two other students in the same situation to determine if there is a deficit or if the behavior is not really a problem

Social skills instruction can include teaching conversation skills, assertiveness, play and peer interaction, problem solving and coping skills, self-help, task-related behaviors, self-concept-related skills (e.g., expressing feelings, accepting consequences), and job-related skills.

One advantage of schooling organizations for students is to facilitate social skills and social development. While teachers cannot take the primary role in developing such traits as honesty, fairness, and concern for others, they are extremely important in the process. The first recommendation is to be a very good role model. As we all know, actions do indeed speak louder than words.

Second, teachers need to communicate expectations and be firm about them. When teachers ignore certain "infractions" and make a big deal about others, they demonstrate to students that it isn't about manners and social skills, but rather discipline and favoritism. All students need to feel safe, cared about, and secure with their classmates. Teachers should be good examples of how to be generous, caring, considerate, and sociable individuals.

Behavior Management Plan Strategies for Increasing Desired Behaviors

1. Prompt: A PROMPT is a visual or verbal cue that assists the child through the behavior-shaping process. In some cases, the teacher may use a physical prompt such as guiding a child's hand. Visual cues include signs or other visual aids. Verbal cues include talking a child through the steps of a task. The gradual removal of the prompt as the child masters the target behavior is called fading.

2. Modeling: In order for modeling to be effective, the child must be at a cognitive and developmental level to imitate the model. Teachers are behavior models in the classroom, but peers are powerful models as well, especially in adolescence. A child who does not perceive a model as acceptable will not likely copy the model's behavior. This is why teachers should be careful

PROMPT: a visual or verbal cue that assists the child through the behavior-shaping process

to reinforce appropriate behavior and not fall into the trap of attending to inappropriate behaviors. Children who see that the students who misbehave get the teacher's constant attention will most likely begin to model those students' behaviors.

3. Contingency contracting: Also known as the Premack Principle or "Grandma's Law," this technique is based on the concept that a less preferred behavior that occurs frequently can be used to increase a preferred behavior that has a lower rate of occurrence. In short, performance of X results in the opportunity to do Y, such as getting 10 minutes of free time for completing the math assignment with 85% accuracy.

   – The use of contingency contracts is a process that continues after formal schooling and into the world of work and adult living. Contracts can be individualized, be developed with input of the child, and accent positive behaviors. Contingencies can also be simple verbal contracts, such as the teacher telling a child that he or she may earn a treat or special activity for completion of a specific academic activity. Contingency contracts can be simple daily contracts or more formal, written contracts.

   – Written contracts last for longer periods of time and must be clear, specific, and fair. Payoffs should be deliverable immediately after the student completes the terms of the contract. An advantage of a written contract is that the child can see and reaffirm the terms of the contract. By being actively involved in the development of the contract with the teacher and/ or parent, the child assumes responsibility for fulfilling his or her share of the deal. Contracts can be renewed and renegotiated as the student progresses toward the target behavior goal.

4. Token Economy: A token economy mirrors the money system in that the students earn tokens (money) that are of little value themselves, but can be traded for tangible or activity rewards, just as currency can be spent for merchandise. Using stamps, stickers, stars, or point cards instead of items like poker chips decrease the likelihood of theft, loss, and noise in the classroom.

   Tips for a token economy:

   – Keep the system simple to understand and administer

   – Develop a reward "menu" that is deliverable and varied

   – Decide on the target behaviors

   – Explain the system completely and in positive terms before beginning the economy

   – Periodically review the rules

— Price the rewards and costs fairly, and post the menu where it can be easily read

— Gradually fade to a variable schedule of reinforcement

Behavior Management Plan Strategies for Decreasing Undesirable Behaviors

1. Extinction: Reinforcement is withheld for an unacceptable behavior. A common example is ignoring the student who calls out without raising his hand and recognizing the student who is raising his hand to speak. This would not be a suitable strategy for serious misbehaviors where others are in danger of being hurt.

2. Differential reinforcement of incompatible behaviors (DRI): In this method, the teacher reinforces an acceptable behavior that is not compatible with the target behavior. A child cannot be out of her seat and in her seat at the same time, so the teacher would reinforce the time when the child is in her seat.

3. Differential reinforcement of alternative behaviors (DRA): The student is rewarded for producing a behavior that is an alternative to the undesired target behavior, such as talking with a classmate instead of arguing.

4. Differential reinforcement of other behaviors (DRO): Reinforcement is provided for producing any appropriate behaviors except for the target behavior during a specified time interval. This technique works well with stereotypic, disruptive, or self-injurious behaviors.

5. Satiation or negative practice: This technique involves reinforcing the inappropriate behavior on a fixed reinforcement schedule until the student discontinues the behavior. The reinforcement must be consistently applied until the student does not want to do it. Behaviors suitable for satiation would be chronic "borrowing" of school supplies or getting up to go to the wastebasket or pencil sharpener. An example of satiation would be giving a student a pencil to sharpen at frequent intervals throughout the day so that the act of getting up to sharpen a pencil no longer has any appeal.

6. Verbal reprimands: Reprimands are best delivered privately, especially for secondary students, who may be provoked into more misbehavior if they are embarrassed in front of their peers. Verbal reprimands also may be a source of attention and reinforcement with some students.

Punishment as a "deterrent" to misbehavior

Punishment should not be the first strategy in behavior management plans because it tends to suppress behavior, not eliminate it. Punishment focuses on the negative rather than positive behaviors. There is also the chance that the child will comply out of fear, stress, or tension rather than a genuine behavior change. Furthermore, the punishment may be misused to the point where it is no longer effective. Forms of punishment include:

1. Adding an aversive event (e.g., detention, lunchroom cleanup, extra assignments)

2. Subtracting something that the child likes (e.g., recess)

   A. Response cost: In token economies, response cost results in loss of points or token. Response-cost or loss of privileges is preferred to adding aversives, but for long-term changes in behavior, punishment is less effective than other forms of decreasing misbehavior, such as extinction and ignoring.

   B. Time-Out: Time-out is removing a child from the reinforcing situation to a setting that is not reinforcing. Time out may be observational (e.g., sitting at the end of the basketball court for five minutes or putting one's head down at the desk). The point is to have the child observe the others engaging in the appropriate behavior.

   – Exclusion time-out: Placing a visual barrier between the student and the rest of the class. This could be a divider between the desks and the time-out area or removing the child to another room.

   – Seclusion time-out: Necessitates a special time-out room that adheres to mandated standards, as well as a log of the children who are taken to time out, the reasons for their removal, and the time they spent there.

In order to be effective, time-out must be consistently applied, and the child must understand why he is being sent to the time out area and for how long. The teacher briefly explains the reason for time-out, directs the child to the area, and refrains from long explanations, arguments, or debates. The time-out area should be as neutral as possible, away from busy areas, and easily observed by the monitor but not the rest of the class. The duration of time-out should vary with the age of the child and timed so the child knows when the end of time-out has arrived.

Time-out as part of a behavior management plan needs to be periodically evaluated for its effectiveness. By analyzing records of time-out (as required and directed by the school district), the teacher can see if the technique is working. If a student regularly goes to time-out at a certain time, the student may be avoiding a frustrating situation or a difficult academic subject. Seclusion time-out may be effective for children who tend to be group-oriented or aggressive and act out frequently. Isolation from the group is not rewarding for them. Shy, solitary, or withdrawn children may actually prefer to be in time-out and may increase the target behavior in order to go to time-out.

3. Overcorrection: Overcorrection is more effective with severe and profoundly handicapped students. The student is required to repeat an appropriate behavior for a specified number of times when the inappropriate behavior is exhibited.

4. Suspension: Suspension is the punishment of last resort. In addition to restrictions on suspension for students with disabilities, suspension translates into a "vacation" from school for many students with behavioral problems. Furthermore, suspension does not relieve the teacher from the responsibility of exploring alternatives that may be effective with the child. An alternative to out-of-school suspension is in-school suspension, where the student is placed in a special area to do his or her class work for a specified time and with minimal privileges. Extended suspensions (i.e., for drugs, weapons, or assault) or offenses punishable by expulsion result in a change of placement, which calls for special meetings to discuss alternative placement and/or services.

Group-Oriented Contingencies in Behavior Management

This strategy uses the power of the peer group to reinforce appropriate behavior. In one variation, dependent group-oriented contingencies, the rewards of consequences for the entire group depend upon the performance of a few members; for example, Susan's class receives a candy reward if she does not have a crying outburst for two days.

Interdependent group-oriented contingencies mean that each member of the group must achieve a specified level of performance in order for the group to get the reward. An example would be the entire class earning one period of free time if everyone passes the science test with at least 80%.

Other strategies for behavior management:

- Counseling techniques: These techniques include life-space interviewing, reality therapy, and active listening

- Realistic consequences: Consequences should be as close as possible to what may happen in the outside world, especially for adolescents

- Student participation: Students, especially older students, should participate as much as possible in the planning, goal setting, and evaluation of their behavior management plans

- Contingency plans: Because adolescents frequently have a number of reinforcers outside of school, the teacher should try to incorporate contingencies for school behavior at home, since parents can control important reinforcers such as movies, going out with friends, car privileges, etc.

- Consistency: Consistency, especially with adolescents, reduces the occurrence of power struggles and teaches them that predictable consequences follow for their choice of actions

Behavior management plan evaluation is a continuous process, because changes in behavior require changes in the target behavior, looking for outside variables that may account for behavior change, or changes in reinforcement schedules and menus.

Initially, the target behavior may increase or worsen as the student realizes that the behavior is no longer reinforced. However, if the behavior management plan is properly administered, the teacher should begin to see results. Behavior management plan evaluation is a continuous process, because changes in behavior require changes in the target behavior, looking for outside variables that may account for behavior change, or changes in reinforcement schedules and menus.

It has already been established that appropriate verbal techniques include a soft, nonthreatening voice; avoidance of undue roughness, anger, or impatience, regardless of whether the teacher is instructing; providing a student alert; or giving a behavior reprimand.

Verbal Techniques and Body Language

Verbal techniques, which may be effective in modifying student behavior, can be as simple as stating the student's name, explaining briefly and succinctly what the student is doing that is inappropriate, and explaining what the student should be doing. Verbal techniques for reinforcing behavior include both encouragement and praise delivered by the teacher.

In addition, for verbal techniques to positively affect student behavior and learning, the teacher must give clear, concise directives while implying her warmth toward the students.

Other factors that contribute to enhanced student learning have to do with body language. The teacher needs to make eye contact with individual students; smile and nod approvingly; move closer to the students; give gentle pats on the shoulder, arm, or head; and bend forward so that the teacher is face to face with the children.

Some of these same techniques can be applied as a means of desisting student misbehaviors. Rather than smiling, the teacher may need to make eye contact first and then shake his or her head disapprovingly. Again, a gentle tap on the shoulder or arm can be used to get a student's attention in an attempt to stop deviancy.

It is also helpful for the teacher to prominently display the classroom rules. This will serve as a visual reminder of the students' expected behaviors. In a study of classroom management procedures, it was established that the combination of conspicuously displayed rules, frequent verbal references to the rules, and appropriate consequences led to increased levels of on-task behavior.

SKILL 9.4 Identify emergency procedures for student and campus safety

Statutes state only the following with regard to school emergencies:

235.14 Emergency drills

The Department of Education shall formulate and prescribe rules and instructions for emergency drills for all the public schools of the state which comprise grades K–12 and for the School for the Deaf and the Blind. Each administrator or teacher in charge of such a facility shall be provided a copy of the rules and instructions; and each such person shall see that such emergency drills are held at least once each calendar quarter and that all personnel and students are properly instructed regarding such rules and instructions.

This statute addresses instructions for drills only—not for actual emergency procedures. Among the possible emergencies that have been identified which schools might face are fire, flood, tornado, bomb threat, chemical accident, traffic-related chemical spill (e.g., Boynton Beach, FL, 1996), earthquake, and hurricane. The primary concern in emergency situations is the physical safety and well being of students. The teacher must be thoroughly familiar with the prescribed movement of students in emergency situations in order to minimize danger to the students and to other school personnel.

See also Skill 9.1

COMPETENCY 10

KNOWLEDGE OF HOW TO PLAN AND CONDUCT LESSONS IN A VARIETY OF LEARNING ENVIRONMENTS THAT LEAD TO STUDENT OUTCOMES CONSISTENT WITH STATE AND DISTRICT STANDARDS

> ### SKILL Determine instructional long-term goals and short-term objectives
> ### 10.1 appropriate to student needs

Once long-range goals have been identified and established, it is important to ensure that all goals and objectives are also in conjunction with student ability and needs. Some objectives may be too basic for a higher-level student, while others cannot be met with a student's current level of knowledge. There are many forms of evaluating student needs to ensure that all goals are challenging, yet achievable.

Teachers should check a student's cumulative file, located in the guidance office, for reading level and prior subject area achievement. This provides a basis for goal setting but shouldn't be the only method used. Depending on the subject area, a basic skills test, reading level evaluations, writing samples, and/or interest surveys can all be useful in determining if all goals are appropriate. Informal observation should always be used as well. Finally, it is important to take into consideration the student's level of motivation when addressing student needs.

When given objectives by the school or county, teachers may wish to adapt them so that they can better meet the needs of their individual student population. For example, if a high-level advanced class is given the objective "*State five causes of World War II,*" a teacher may wish to adapt the objective to a higher level: "*State five causes of World War II and explain how they contributed to the start of the war.*" Objectives can be modified for a lower level as well: "*From a list of causes, pick three that specifically caused World War II.*"

When organizing and sequencing objectives, the teacher needs to remember that skills are building blocks. A taxonomy of educational objectives can be helpful to construct and organize objectives. Knowledge of material—for example, memorizing definitions or famous quotes—is low on the taxonomy of learning and should be worked with early in the sequence of teaching. Eventually, objectives should be developed to include higher-level thinking such as comprehension (i.e., being able to use a definition), application (i.e., being able to apply the definition to other situations), synthesis (i.e., being able to add other information), and evaluation (i.e., being able to judge the value of something).

EMERGENT CURRICULUM describes the projects and themes that classrooms may embark upon that have been inspired by the children's interests. The teacher uses all the tools of assessment available to her to learn as much as she can about her students and then she continually assesses them over the period of the unit or semester. As she gets to know them, she listens to what their interests are and creates a curriculum in response to what she learns from her observations of her own students.

Webbing is a recent concept related to the idea of emergent curriculum. The two main uses of webbing are planning and recording curriculum. Planning webs are used to generate ideas for activities and projects for the children from an observed interest such as rocks.

Teachers work together to come up with ideas and activities for the children and to record them in a web format. Activities can be grouped by different areas of the room or by developmental domains. For example, clusters either fall under areas, such as dramatic play or science, or around domains, such as language, cognitive, and physical development. Either configuration works; being consistent in each web is important.

This format will work as a unit, weekly, or monthly program plan. Any new activities that emerge throughout the unit can also be added to the web. The record will help to plan in the future, using activities that emerge from the children's play and ideas.

SKILL 10.2 Identify activities that support the knowledge, skills, and attitudes to be learned in a given subject area

As a teacher, it is important to be aware of the skills and information that are pertinent to the subject area being taught. Teachers need to determine what information a student should carry with them at the end of a term. The teacher should also be aware of skills needed to complete any objective for that subject area and determine how advanced their students are at using them.

Because most goals are building blocks, all necessary underlying skills should be determined and a teacher must evaluate if the student has demonstrated these abilities. For example, to do mathematical word problems, students must have a sufficiently high reading level to understand the problem.

OBJECTIVE: a specific learning outcome that is used to achieve long-range goals

Once the desired knowledge, skills, and attitudes have been established, a teacher must develop short-range objectives designed to help in the achievement of these outcomes. An **OBJECTIVE** is a specific learning outcome that is used to achieve long-range goals. Objectives should be stated in observable terms, such as *to state, to demonstrate, to list, to complete,* or *to solve.* Objectives should be clear and concise (e.g.. students will be able to state five causes of World War II).

SKILL 10.3 Identify materials based on instructional objectives and student learning needs and performance levels

In considering suitable learning materials for the classroom, the teacher must have a thorough understanding of the state-mandated competency-based curriculum. According to state requirements, certain objectives must be met in each subject taught at every designated level of instruction. It is necessary that the teacher become well acquainted with the curriculum for which he or she is assigned. The teacher must also be aware that it is unlawful to require students to study from textbooks or materials other than those approved by the State Department of Education.

Keeping in mind the state requirements concerning the objectives and materials, the teacher must determine the abilities of the incoming students assigned to his or her class or supervision. It is essential to be aware of their entry behavior—that is, their current level of achievement in the relevant areas. The next step is to take a broad overview of students who are expected to learn before they are passed on to the next grade or level of instruction. Finally, the teacher must design a course of study that will enable students to reach the necessary level of achievement as displayed in their final assessments, or exit behaviors. Textbooks and learning materials must be chosen to fit into this context.

To determine the abilities of incoming students, it may be helpful to consult their prior academic records. Letter grades assigned at previous levels of instruction as well as scores on standardized tests may be taken into account. In addition, the teacher may choose to administer pretests at the beginning of the school year, and perhaps also at the initial stage of each new unit of instruction. The textbooks available for classroom use may provide suitable pre-tests, tests of student progress, and post-tests.

Selecting Assessments

In selecting tests and other assessment tools, the teacher should keep in mind that different kinds of tests measure different aspects of student development. The tests included in most textbooks chosen for the classroom and in the teacher's manual that accompanies them are usually achievement tests. Few of these are the type of tests intended to measure the students' inherent ability or aptitude. Teachers will find it difficult to raise students' scores on ability tests, but students' scores on achievement tests may be expected to improve with proper instruction and application in the area being studied.

In addition to administering tests, the teacher may assess the readiness of students for a particular level of instruction by having them demonstrate their ability to perform some relevant task. In a class that emphasizes written composition, for example, students may be asked to submit writing samples.

These may be used not only to ensure that the students are placed into the proper level, but also as a diagnostic tool to help them understand what aspects of their composition skills may need improvement. In the like manner, students in a speech class may be asked to make an impromptu oral presentation before beginning a specific level of instruction. Others may be asked to demonstrate their psychomotor skills in a physical education class, display their computational skills in a mathematics class, and so on. Whatever the chosen task, the teacher will need to select or devise an appropriate assessment scale and interpret the results with care.

If students are informed of their entry behaviors on such a scale, they will be better motivated, especially if they are able to observe their progress by an objective means at suitable intervals during the course. For this reason, it may be advisable to record the results of such assessments in the student's portfolios as well as in the teacher's records.

Teachers may also gauge student readiness by simply asking them about their previous experience or knowledge of the subject or task at hand. While their comments may not be completely reliable indicators of what they know or understand, such discussions have the advantage of providing an idea of the students' interest in what is being taught. Teachers can have little impact unless they are able to demonstrate how the material being introduced is relevant to the students' lives.

Keeping in mind what is understood about the students' abilities and interests, the teacher should design a course of study that presents units of instruction in an orderly sequence. The instruction should be planned to advance all students toward the next level of instruction, although exit behaviors need not be identical due to the inevitability of individual differences.

Selecting Learning Materials

Once students' abilities are determined, the teacher will select the learning materials for the class. In choosing materials, teachers should also keep in mind that not only do students learn at different rates, but they bring a variety of cognitive styles to the learning process. Prior experiences influence the individual's COGNITIVE STYLE, or method of accepting, processing, and retaining information.

COGNITIVE STYLE: method of accepting, processing, and retaining information

Most teachers choose to use textbooks that are suitable to the age and developmental level of specific student populations. Textbooks reflect the values and assumptions of the society that produces them, while they also represent the knowledge and skills considered to be essential in becoming an educated adult. Finally, textbooks are useful to the school bureaucracy and the community because they make public and accessible the private world of the classroom.

Though these factors may favor the adoption of textbooks, the individual teacher may have only limited choice about which textbooks to use, since such decisions are often made by the school administration or the local school district (in observance of the state guidelines). Even if teachers are consulted about textbook selection, it is likely that they have little training in evaluation techniques, and they are seldom granted leave time to encourage development of such informed decisions. On those occasions when teachers are asked to assist in the selection process, they should ask, above all, whether the textbooks have real substance—is World War II accurately chronicled, does the science textbook correctly conceptualize electrical current, do literary selections reflect a full range of genres?

From time to time, controversy has arisen about the possible weakness of textbooks—the preponderance of pictures and illustrations, the avoidance of controversy in social studies textbooks, the lack of emphasis on problem-solving in science books, and so on. In the 1980s, certain books were criticized for their attention to the liberal or secular values, and the creationism/evolution argument has resurfaced again and again.

Finally, recent decades have witnessed a movement to grant more attention to women, African-Americans, and other groups whose contributions to our developing culture may have been overlooked in earlier textbooks. Individual teachers would be well advised to keep themselves informed of current trends or developments so as to make better-informed choices for their students and deal with the possibility of parental concern.

Focusing on the needs evident in almost any classroom population, the teacher will want to use textbooks that include some of the activities and selections to challenge the most advanced students as well as those who have difficulty in mastering the material at a moderate pace. Some of the exercises may be eliminated altogether for faster learners, while students who have difficulty may need to have material arranged into brief steps or sections.

For almost any class, some experience in cooperative learning may be advisable. Thus, the faster learners will reinforce what they have already mastered, while those of lesser ability at the tasks in question can ask about their individual problems or areas of concern. Most textbook exercises intended for independent work can be used in cooperative learning, though in most cases, teachers will encourage better participation if the cooperating group is asked to hand in a single paper or project to represent their combined efforts, rather than individual papers or projects. This method does not always require that all members of the group be assigned the same grade (if letter grades are assigned at all for such assignments).

Depending on what students have been told before starting the activity, the teacher may be justified in adjusting grades accordingly if she observes some students applying more effort than the others to the cooperative learning endeavor.

In choosing materials, teachers should also keep in mind that students learn at different rates and bring a variety of cognitive styles to the learning process. Prior experiences influence the individual's cognitive style, or method of accepting, processing, and retaining information. According to Marshall Rosenberg, students can be categorized as:

- Rigid-inhibited

- Undisciplined

- Acceptance-anxious

- Creative

"The creative learner is an independent thinker, one who maximizes his/her abilities, can work by his/herself, enjoys learning, and is self-critical" (Rosenberg). This last category constitutes the ideal, but teachers should make every effort to use materials that will stimulate and hold the attention of learners of all types.

Aside from textbooks, there is a wide variety of materials available to today's teachers. Computers are now commonplace, and some schools can now afford DVDs to bring alive the content of a reference book in text, motion, and sound. Hand-held calculators eliminate the need for drill and practice in number facts, while they also support a problem-solving process for mathematics. Videocassette recorders and DVD players are common and permit the use of home-produced or commercially produced tapes. Textbook publishers often provide films, recordings, and software to accompany the text, as well as maps, graphics, and colorful posters to help students visualize what is being taught.

Teachers can usually scan the educational publishers' brochures that arrive at their principal's or department head's office on a frequent basis. Another way to stay current in the field is by attending workshops or conferences. Teachers will be enthusiastically welcomed on those occasions when educational publishers are asked to display their latest productions and revised editions of materials.

In addition, yesterday's libraries are today's media centers. Teachers can usually have opaque projectors delivered to the classroom to project print or pictorial images (including student work) onto a screen for classroom viewing. Some teachers have chosen to replace chalkboards with transparency projectors that reproduce the print or images. These can easily be stored for later use. In an art or photography class, or any class in which it is helpful to display visual materials, slides can easily be projected onto a wall or a screen. Cameras are inexpensive enough to enable students to photograph and display their own work, as well as keep a record of their achievements in teacher files or student portfolios.

COMPETENCY 11
KNOWLEDGE OF COLLABORATIVE STRATEGIES FOR WORKING WITH VARIOUS EDUCATION PROFESSIONALS, PARENTS, AND OTHER APPROPRIATE PARTICIPANTS IN THE CONTINUAL IMPROVEMENT OF EDUCATIONAL EXPERIENCES OF STUDENTS

SKILL 11.1 Identify student behavior indicating possible emotional distress, substance abuse, abuse or neglect, and suicidal tendencies

Emotional Stress and Abuse

Because all children experience stressful periods within their lives from time to time, all students may demonstrate some behaviors that indicate emotional distress. Emotionally healthy students can maintain control of their own behavior even during stressful times. The difference between typical stress-response behavior and severe emotional distress is determined by the frequency, duration, and intensity of stress-responsive behavior.

Signs of emotional distress

Lying, stealing, and fighting are maladaptive behaviors that any children may exhibit occasionally; however, if a child lies, steals, or fights regularly or blatantly, then these behaviors may be indicative of emotional distress. Lying can be especially common among young children who do so to avoid punishment or as a means to make themselves feel more important. As they move out of early childhood, lying can be a signal that children are feeling insecure. If feelings of insecurity escalate, lying may become habitual or obvious and that may indicate that the child is seeking attention because of emotional distress. Fighting, especially among siblings, is a common occurrence. However, if a child fights constantly, is unduly aggressive, or is belligerent toward others on a long-term basis, teachers and parents need to consider the possibility of emotional problems.

It is imperative that teachers are able to identify when children need help with their behavior, therefore, educators must constantly monitor student behaviors; it is through their own actions that children will indicate that they need and/or want help. Repeatedly breaking established rules or destroying property can signify that a student is losing control. Other signs that a child needs help may include frequent bouts of crying, a quarrelsome attitude, and constant complaints about school, friends, or life in general. Any time a child's disposition, attitude, or habits change significantly, teachers and parents must seriously consider emotional difficulties.

> *It is imperative that teachers are able to identify when children need help with their behavior, therefore, educators must constantly monitor student behaviors; it is through their own actions that children will indicate that they need and/or want help.*

Addressing emotionally distressed students

Classroom teachers have many safe and helpful interventions to assist them with students who are suffering serious emotional disturbances. First, the teacher must communicate the nature and extent of the suspected issues. Next, the school involves other professionals and parents/guardians in order to provide an appropriate safety net for the intervention. This is done unless the parents/guardians are suspected as the source of abuse. Finally, two-way communication constantly flows between the home and school, on a daily basis if necessary, to ensure that the student has a successful transition back to appropriate thoughts and behaviors.

By establishing environments that promote appropriate behavior for all students, teachers can reduce negative behaviors in the classroom. First, clear rules must be established and should include the understanding that students are to have respect for one another. If necessary, classmates may need to be informed of a student's special needs so they can give due consideration. For instance, if a student is blind, the teacher will need to explain the disability and specify that students keep the room in order at all times so that their classmate can navigate.

Behavior modification programs

For any student who might show emotional or behavioral disorders, a BEHAVIOR MODIFICATION PROGRAM is usually effective. Severe disorders may require that on a regular basis a school psychologist, guidance counselor, or behavior specialist is directly involved with the student and provides counseling and therapy. Frequently such interventions also involve the student's family. If deviant behavior does occur, the teacher should have a plan of action to difuse the situation and protect the student and other individuals. Such a plan could include a safe and secure time-out place where the student can go to regain self-control.

If a behavior disorder is very severe, the student may need to be involved in a more concentrated program aimed at alleviating deviant behavior, such as psychotherapy. In such instances, the school psychologist, guidance counselor, or behavior specialist is directly involved with the student and provides counseling and therapy on a regular basis. These staff members may also need to keep regular contact with the student's family.

As a last resort, some families are turning to drug therapy. Once viewed as a radical step, administering drugs to children to balance their emotions or control their behavior has become a widely used form of therapy. Of course, only a medical doctor can prescribe such drugs.

Great care must be exercised when giving pills to children in order to change their behavior, especially because so many medicines have undesirable side effects. It is important to know that these drugs relieve only the symptoms of behavior and do not get at the underlying causes. Parents and teachers need to be educated about the side effects of these medications.

> **BEHAVIOR MODIFICA-TION PROGRAM:** a course of action designed to help a student deal with emotional or behavioral disorders

Neurotic Disorders

Emotional disorders can escalate so severely that the child's well-being is threatened. Teachers and parents must recognize the signs of severe emotional stress, which may become detrimental to the child and others. During childhood, of the various forms of emotional disorders, neurotic disorders are the second most common group. Physical symptoms of NEUROSES include:

- Extreme or ongoing anxiety
- Overdependence
- Social isolation
- Sleep problems

- Nausea
- Abdominal pain
- Diarrhea
- Headaches

Children may also have irrational fears of particular objects or situations or become consumed with obsessions, thoughts, or ideas. One of the most serious neuroses is depression. Signs that a child is depressed include:

> **NEUROSIS:** a psychological disorder that is characterized by general distress

- Ongoing sadness

- Crying

- Lack of interest in people or activities

- Eating and sleep disorders

- Talking about wanting to be dead

Teachers and other adults must listen to what the child is saying and should take these verbal expressions very seriously. Many schoolhouse tragedies, including those in Columbine, Colorado; Jonesboro, Arkansas; and Lake Worth, Florida, may have been prevented if the signs of emotional distress had been recognized and resolved.

Psychotic Disorders

Even more serious than neurosis is PSYCHOSIS, which is characterized by a loss of contact with reality. Psychosis is rare in childhood, but when it does occur, it is often difficult to diagnose. One fairly constant sign is failure to make normal emotional contact with other people. With schizophrenia, a common psychosis of childhood, the individual deliberately escapes from reality and withdraws from relationships with others. This disorder can be described as a person having contact with others, but through a curtain. Schizophrenia is more common in boys than in girls; a major hallmark is a habitually flat or agitated facial expression. Children suffering from schizophrenia are occasionally mute, but at times they talk incessantly using bizarre words in ways that make no sense. In a vicious cycle, their incoherent speech contributes to their frustration, and this compounds their fears and preoccupation.

PSYCHOSIS: a psychological disorder that is characterized by a loss of contact with reality

Early Infantile Autism

The cause of EARLY INFANTILE AUTISM is unknown. In the past, some psychiatrists speculated that these children did not develop normally due to a lack of parental warmth. This has been dismissed as unlikely because the incidence of autism in families is usually limited to one child. While there are no scientific confirmations, some theorize that the disorder may be caused by metabolic or chromosomal defects.

EARLY INFANTILE AUTISM: a disorder that is characterized by impaired social interaction and communication

Signs of early infantile autism

Early infantile autism may occur as early as the fourth month of life and may present itself as an infant lying apathetically and oblivious in the crib. In other cases, the baby appears to develop at a normal pace throughout infancy only to have the symptoms appear without warning at about eighteen months of age. Due to the nature of the symptoms, autistic children are often misdiagnosed as mentally retarded, deaf-mute, or organically brain-damaged. With this disorder as well, boys are twice as likely as girls to be diagnosed.

According to many psychologists who have been involved with treating autistic children, it seems that these children have built a wall between themselves and everyone else, including their families, and even their parents. They do not make eye contact with others and do not even appear to hear the voices of those who speak to them. They cannot empathize with others and have no ability to appreciate humor.

Autistic children usually have language disturbances. One third never develop any speech; however, they may grunt or whine. Others may repeat the same word or phrase over and over or "parrot" what someone else has said. They often lack inner-language and cannot play by themselves above a primitive, sensory-motor level.

Frequently, autistic children will develop a preoccupation with objects; this appears to fill the void left by the absence of interpersonal relationships. They become compulsive about the arrangements of objects and often engage in simple, repetitive physical activities with objects for long periods of time. If these activities are interrupted, they may react with fear or rage. Others remain motionless for hours each day sometimes moving only their eyes or hands.

Socialization of autistic children

The developmental abilities of autistic children varies greatly. On intelligence tests they may score from severely subnormal to high average. Some exhibit astonishing abilities in isolated skill areas; for instance, one child may memorize volumes of material, another might sing beautifully, and a third might perform complicated mathematical problems. This phenomenon was popularized by the movie *Rainman*.

The prognosis for autistic children is painfully discouraging. Only about five percent of autistic children become socially well adjusted in adulthood. Another twenty percent make fair social adjustments. The remaining seventy-five percent are socially incapacitated and must be supervised for the duration of their lives.

Treatment may include outpatient psychotherapy, drugs, or long-term treatment in a residential center; however, for the long term, neither the presence nor absence of treatment appears to make a difference.

Behaviors Indicating Drug/Alcohol Abuse

Legally, the use of any illicit substance by a minor, including alcohol, is automatically considered abuse. This issue must be tackled by educators because illegal substances hamper and reduce social and academic functioning. The adage "Pot makes a smart kid average and an average kid dumb" is quite accurate with almost every controlled substance. There exist not a few families where substance abuse, such as pot smoking, is a known habit of the parents. Parental use hampers national drug and alcohol prevention efforts because children may start their dependency by stealing from parents. In addition, parental use negates the message that substance abuse is wrong.

Stages of substance abuse

Substance abuse, regardless of the substance, follows a pattern of withdrawal, blackouts, and tolerance. WITHDRAWAL occurs when the substance is removed from the blood stream and a metabolic craving is accompanied by:

- Sweating
- Nausea
- Dizziness
- Elevated blood pressure
- Seizures
- Death (in rare instances)

During the BLACKOUT stage an abuser experiences serious physical symptoms but later doesn't remember anything of his actions. The anesthetized mind has eliminated conscious wakeful activity, functioning mainly on instinct. TOLERANCE is the final stage and changes over the course of the disease, increasing in the early stages and decreasing in the late chronic stage.

Dangers of unaddressed substance abuse

In the school setting, hard signs of dependency are rare and, when seen, they must be considered very serious. Due to the danger of long-term injury or fatality, substance ingestion must be treated immediately by medical staff. Fatalities can occur in cases of seizures due to withdrawal, overdoses due to mixing substances, or overuse of a single substance including overdoses with alcohol alone. Never, under any circumstances, attempt to treat, protect, tolerate, or negotiate with a student who is showing signs of a physical crisis. It is advisable to find out the protocol for a particular school or district; however, most schools require the student to be isolated until they are removed from the school center by EMS or police.

Abuse versus dependency

While there is a difference between abuse and dependency, for this age group they can be viewed in the same light. This is particularly true because for young people, addiction occurs at a high rate, rapidly after first use, and sometimes after only a few tries. Abuse is a lesser degree of involvement with substances; usually implying the person is not physically addicted. They may have just as many "soft signs" of involvement but lack true addiction. Dependency indicates a true physical addiction, characterized by several hard signs, some of which are less likely to be seen in a school setting. When deprived of the substance, the person may experience withdrawal symptoms, blackouts, tolerance, irresponsibility, and illogical

WITHDRAWAL: a stage of substance abuse when the substance is removed from the blood stream causing a metabolic craving

BLACKOUT: a stage of substance abuse when an abuser experiences serious physical symptoms but later doesn't remember anything of his actions

TOLERANCE: the final stage of substance abuse characterized by a resistance to the effects of the substance

In the school setting, hard signs of dependency are rare and when seen, they must be considered very serious.

behavior. Soft signs include declines in functioning in all domains including social and occupational, mental and emotional, and spiritual life.

Social signs of substance abuse

Social decline is one of the signs of drug or alcohol abuse. In being acquainted with all students, educators will notice personality changes in any student. Characteristically, social withdrawal is first noticed when the student fails to say hello, avoids being near teachers, seems evasive or sneaky, and associates with a different, less academically focused, group of friends. Obviously, association with known substance abusers is almost always a warning sign. Adults must not accept the explanation that the suspected abuser is just being friends with the known abuser, or that the suspected abuser has many kinds of friends. There is a sharp demarcation between youth who abuse substances and those who do not. Typically, a young person does not straddle the line unless they intend to "hop the fence" once in a while.

> There is a sharp demarcation between youth who abuse substances and those who do not. Typically, a young person does not straddle the line unless they intend to "hop the fence" once in a while.

The abuser will progressively disregard their appearance, showing up unclean, unkempt, and disheveled. Actual style of fashion may change to more radical trends such as nose rings, body piercings, and tattoos. Such fashion choices are used by nonabusing youth and, on their own, are not an indication of substance abuse; however, there does seem to be a high correlation. The socially impaired substance abuser will frequently be late for school, classes, and other appointments. The abuser seeks less and less satisfaction from traditional social activities such as school athletics, rallies, plays, student government, and after-school programs. In contrast, some abusers hide behind conformity, going to great pains to appear normal; these may be some of the most seriously impaired of all.

Mental/emotional signs of substance abuse

Mental and emotional impairments manifest as the addiction deepens. Academic indicators include declining school performance, standardized test scores, and interest in school. In addition, students with addictions may:

- Respond more slowly to prompts, sharp noises, or sudden actions

- Show emotional flattening and personality changes

- Have vacant expressions, hyperactivity, depression, psychosis, and a lack of motivation

- Discuss or attempt suicide

Students already having emotional problems (about three to six percent of any given population of youth) are more vulnerable to using drugs and alcohol than students who are well adjusted. Caution is recommended when educators question teenagers to ascertain drug and alcohol abuse. Students might have another psychiatric illness of which the school is not aware. They may appear to be high or intoxicated; but instead, they may be reacting to medications. Their odd behavior may be due to the psychiatric illness itself, not substance abuse. Thus, whenever possible, it is helpful to know a student's history.

Spiritual signs of substance abuse

The last step is spiritual decline, an even less obvious manifestation than the other signs of substance abuse. The broadest definition of SPIRITUALITY is the youth's existential relationship to the greater world. Attitudes of respect, humility, wonder, and affection indicate a person who has a sense of relationship to something greater. Attitudes of contempt, pride, ignorance, and arrogance indicate one who lacks an awareness of the enormity of existence. More specifically, a previously religious or reverent student may suddenly become blatantly disrespectful of organized religion. The inappropriate use of the cross or other religious symbol may also indicate spiritual decline.

> **SPIRITUALITY:** the youth's existential relationship to the greater world

Reasons for substance abuse

Although most students understand the dangers of drug and alcohol use, hardcore users cannot resist involvement. They may disregard the dangers because their emotional pain is so high. In today's complex world, many factors lead to high levels of emotional pain, not the least of which is family and community breakdown. Today, the divorce rate is extremely high and approximately one half of families are blended. Children are transported from parent to parent, often against their own wishes, and ex-spouses may retaliate against each other through children. Children from these families feel guilt, anger, and shame, feelings that can be dangerous as they usually remain unresolved. Once considered relatively harmless to children, divorce is now being reevaluated and is now viewed as a serious challenge.

Other causes of emotional pain include:

- Social awkwardness
- Depression
- Undiagnosed and/or untreated mental illnesses
- Personality disorders
- Learning disabilities
- ADHD
- Conduct disorders
- Substance abuse and dependency in family members

The most common manifestation of emotional pain are parent–child issues, which include deficits in communication, authority, and respect between parent(s) and child(ren). An equally common signal of emotional issues is conduct disorders, a behavior set characterized by:

- Aggression
- Exploitation
- Violence
- Disregard for the rights of others
- Animal cruelty
- Fire-setting
- Bed-wetting

- Defiance
- Running away
- Truancy
- Juvenile arrest records
- ADHD
- Substance abuse

SKILL 11.2 Identify school and community resources and collaborative procedures to meet the intellectual, personal, and social needs of all students

Teachers should create personalized learning communities where every student is a valued member and contributor of the classroom experiences. In classrooms where socio-cultural attributes of the student population are incorporated into the fabric of the learning process, dynamic interrelationships are created that enhance the learning experience and the personalization of learning. Everyone in the classroom benefits from bonding through shared experiences and having an expanded view of a culture that vastly differs from their own.

In order to create personalized learning communities, educators must use information from the school experience to create relationships that forge bridges of collaboration between school resources and community resources. The interaction chart of personalized learning shows the research of Clarke and Frazer (2003) in evaluating the developmental needs for students in school communities.

INTERACTIONS IN PERSONALIZED LEARNING		
Personal Needs	**Relationships**	**School Practices**
Self-expression	Recognition from school	Provides equity
Creating self-identity	Acceptance—feeling of belonging	Shared community
Choosing one's own path	Creating trust	Range of options for student development
Freedom to take risks	Respect from community	Taking responsibility
Using one's imagination to view self projections	Fulfilling one's purpose in life	Creating greater challenges
Successful mastery	Confirm one's progress and goals	Having clear expectations for performance

In a personalized learning community, students must feel a sense of connection to teachers and staff. Teachers know students by name and individual expression. Greeting students in the morning with names and a special recognition, such as "Jamie, thanks for participating the school's recycling program," or "Great job, David, in that last quarter touchdown at last Friday's football game," will go a long way in creating an affirming and connected school environment.

Researchers continue to show that personalized learning environments increase the learning effect for students; decrease drop-out rates among marginalized students; and decrease unproductive student behavior, which can result from constant cultural misunderstandings or miscues between students. Promoting diversity of learning and cultural competency in the classroom for students and teachers creates a world of multicultural opportunities and learning. When students are able to step outside their comfort zones and share themselves, then students grow exponentially in social understanding and cultural connectedness.

Students who feel like they belong in their school communities may feel motivated to succeed academically more than students who simply feel like "just a number" among the thousands of students. Parents and community members who are actively involved in Parent Student Teacher Associations (PTSAs) and community after-school support groups will find that students actually appreciate having their support and involvement in school activities and governance.

Community support provides additional resources for classrooms and school communities on limited district budgets. Additional grant sources from local PTSAs and educational organizations continue to provide financial resources for teachers seeking to provide maximal learning opportunities for students.

SKILL 11.3 Identify the rights, legal responsibilities, and procedures for reporting incidences of abuse or neglect or other signs of distress

All schools have guidelines for teachers receiving assistance in obtaining resources for students with special needs, especially since the implementation of the Americans with Disabilities Act. The first step in securing help is for the teacher to approach the school's administration or exceptional education department with a request for additional resources. Many schools have a committee designated for addressing these needs, such as a Child Study Team or Core Team. These teams are made up of regular and special education teachers, school psychologists, guidance counselors, and administrators. The particular student's classroom teacher usually has to complete some initial paper work and will need to complete some behavioral observations.

The teacher will take this information to the appropriate committee for discussion and consideration. The committee will recommend the next step to be taken. Subsequent steps may include a complete psychological evaluation along with certain physical examinations, such as vision and hearing screening and a complete medical examination by a doctor.

The referral of students for this process is usually relatively simple for the classroom teacher and requires little more than some initial paper work and discussion. The services and resources the student receives as a result of the process typically prove to be invaluable to the student with behavioral disorders.

At times, the teacher must go beyond the school system to meet the needs of some students. An awareness of special services and resources and how to obtain them is essential to all teachers and their students. When the school system is unable to address the needs of a student, the teacher must take the initiative and contact agencies within the community.

SKILL 11.4 Apply knowledge of the contents of, and the procedures for maintaining, permanent student records

The student permanent record is a file of the student's cumulative educational history. It contains a profile of the student's academic background as well as the student's behavioral and medical background. Other pertinent individual information contained in the permanent record includes the student's attendance, grade averages, and schools attended. Personal information such as parents' names and addresses, immunization records, child's height and weight, and narrative information about the child's progress and physical and mental well being is an important aspect of the permanent record. All information contained within the permanent record is strictly confidential and is only to be discussed with the student's parents or other involved school personnel.

The purpose of the permanent record is to provide applicable information about the student so that the student's individual educational needs can be met. If any specialized testing has been administered, the results are noted in the permanent record. Any special requirements that the student may have are indicated in the permanent record. Highly personal information, including court orders regarding custody, is filed in the permanent record as is appropriate. The importance and value of the permanent record cannot be underestimated. It offers a comprehensive knowledge of the student.

The current teacher is responsible for maintaining the student's permanent record. All substantive information in regard to testing, academic performance, the student's medical condition, and personal events are placed in the permanent record file. Updated information in regard to the student's grades, attendance, and behavior is added annually. These files are kept in a locked fireproof room or file cabinet and cannot be removed from this room unless the person removing them signs a form acknowledging full responsibility for the safe return of the complete file. Again, only the student's parents (or legal guardians), the teacher, or other concerned school personnel may view the contents of the permanent record file.

The permanent record file follows the student as he or she moves through the school system. Anytime the student leaves a school, the permanent record is transferred with the student. The permanent record is regarded as legal documentation of a student's educational experience.

SKILL 11.5 Identify the role of teachers on collaborative teams *(e.g., IEP, 504, AIP, and child study)*

See Skill 7.5

SKILL 11.6 Interpret statewide criterion-referenced assessment data for parents with only rudimentary knowledge of assessment terms and concepts

Student performance criterion-referenced data assessments are used to answer questions such as, "Are students learning?" and "How well are students learning?" These assessments provide parents with a quantifiable response to these questions.

The National Study of School Evaluation (NSSE) 1997 research paper, "School Improvement: Focusing on Student Performance," adds the following questions for evaluating student learning outcomes:

- What are the types of assessments of student learning that are used in the school?

- What do the results of the data assessments indicate about the current levels of student learning performance? About future predictions? What were the learning objectives and goals?

- What are the strengths and limitations in student learning and achievement?

- How prepared are students for further education or promotion to the next level of education?

- What are the trends seen in student learning in various subject areas or overall academic learning?

At each grade level, the FCAT (Florida Comprehensive Assessment Test) uses the same testing format and scoring for subject areas tested in Reading, Mathematics, Science, and Writing. The scale scores range from 100–500 points. Developmental scores noting the annual progress of students are also given with the actual student scores on each section of the testing process. The developmental scores are given from grade to grade level and range from 86 to 3008, so a student taking the test as a 10th grader in 2006 would have a developmental score of 2006. The range of testing scores includes the following:

- High range: 400–500

- Middle range: 325–399

- Low range: 130–324

Students who received scores in the high range in each testing subject area can receive Certificates of Achievement that demonstrate outstanding or notable performances on the Florida Sunshine State Standards. At each grade level of the FCAT, the topic areas are the same; so in Science, for example, the tested areas would be:

- Physical and Chemical Science

- Earth and Space Sciences

- Life and Environmental Sciences

- Scientific Thinking

Providing parents with opportunities to attend in-service workshops on data discussions with teachers and administrators creates additional opportunity for parents to ask questions and become actively involved in monitoring their student's educational progress. With state assessments, parents should look for the words "passed" or "met/exceeded standards" in interpreting the numerical data on student reports.

SKILL 11.7 Interpret national norm-referenced assessment data for parents with only rudimentary knowledge of assessment terms and concepts

The Florida Department of Education uses a variety of norm-referenced tests (NRTs) to assess student learning performances. The tests vary in content and assessment knowledge, so they are not interchangeable or comparative between schools and districts. The listing of tests below includes a comprehensive report on the number of students tested and the median national percentile ranking (NPR) of comparative student performance to students in a defined norm group of testers. The NPR is ranked from 1 to 99, where an NPR of 40 means that a student scored the same as or better than 40% of the students testing nationally.

For the parent who is interpreting NPR assessments, the rule of thumb is that typically 25% of the students test in the lower range of 1–25 and 25% of the students test in the higher range of 76–99; these statistics represent a low and high testing ranking of all test takers nationally. The majority of students test in the range of 26–75.

FLORIDA NRTS,1995–1997, GRADES 4 & 8	
ABBREVIATION	**TEST**
CAT A	California Achievement Test Form A
CAT E/F	California Achievement Test Forms E & F
CTB A/B	Comprehensive Test of Basic Skills Forms A and B
CTB U/V	Comprehensive Test of Basic Skills Forms U and V
ITB K	Iowa Test of Basic Skills Form K
NAT 3	Comprehensive Assessment Program National Achievement Test Form 3
STA E/F	Stanford Achievement Test Forms E and F
STA J/K/L	Stanford Achievement Test Forms J,K & L

In looking at actual NRT test results from five Florida school districts, parents can see student performance in reading and mathematics, which may then help in determining trends and predictions of student learning outcomes in school communities. The NRT Grade 8 report for 1997 testing results was taken directly from the Florida Assessment Reports for five school districts in evaluating student performance in reading and mathematics.

NORM-REFERENCED TEST REPORT GRADE 8 REPORT - 1997										
			READING				**MATHEMATICS**			
District	**Test**		**No. of Students**	**Median NPR**	**Percent in Each NPR Group**		**No. of Students**	**Median NPR**	**Percent in Each NPR Group**	
					1-25	**76-99**			**1-25**	**76-99**
ALACHUA	ITB	K	1756	54	22	31	1754	54	25	27
BAKER	CTB	A	248	55	19	28	249	60	18	30
BAY	CAT	A	1488	56	16	27	1482	60	17	30
BRADFORD	CTB	A	217	53	25	23	216	46	25	18
BREVARD	STA	J	3980	57	19	27	3873	58	18	29

For example, in the Alachua District, there were 1,756 students taking the reading tests. Of those students, the median NPR range was 54 percent scored in the range from 26–75, with 22 percent of students testing in the lower range of 1–25, and 31 percent of students testing in the higher range of 76–99, all of which typifies the NRT testing results.

Evaluating the math rankings yields comparable ranking results for students taking the ITB test. What parents can ascertain is that the results for the Districts 2-5 is that there were a variety of tests given to assess student learning that ranged from the CTB to the STA norm-reference testing, so the tests cannot be compared to each other because their contents were developed to assess specific student learning outcomes.

Parents must look at the complete student portfolio—including specific subject area progress reports, discipline records, attendance, student/teacher logs on in-class performance, and predicted final grade outcome—before making definitive judgments on student learning in school communities. NRT data is only one type of assessment that provides parents with reference information on student academic performance, so parents must reserve judgment until a complete portfolio is obtained from both teachers and students in classrooms.

COMPETENCY 12
KNOWLEDGE OF STRATEGIES FOR THE IMPLEMENTATION OF TECHNOLOGY IN THE TEACHING AND LEARNING PROCESS

SKILL 12.1 Identify appropriate software to prepare materials, deliver instruction, assess student achievement, and manage classroom tasks

With a surplus of educational software on the market, it is important for an educator to be able to evaluate a program before purchasing it. Software can vary greatly in content, presentation, skill level, and objectives. If a teacher is in the position of having to purchase a computer program for use in the classroom without any prior knowledge of the program itself, it is useful to have some guidelines to follow.

Once a program has been purchased and the shrink-wrap has been removed, many vendors are reluctant to allow its return because of a possible violation of copyright laws or damage to the software medium. For this reason it is important to preview the software personally before buying it. If a vendor is reluctant to allow the teacher to preview a program prior to its purchase, it is sometimes possible to get a preview copy from the publisher.

Many school districts have addressed this problem by publishing a list of approved software titles for each grade level in much the same way that they publish lists of approved textbooks and other classroom materials. In addition, most districts have developed a software evaluation form to be used by any instructor involved in the purchase of software that is not already on the "approved" list. Use of a software evaluation form can eliminate a lot of the risk involved when shopping for appropriate titles for the classroom. In many districts, all software is evaluated by the actual instructors that will use the software, and the completed evaluation forms are made available for the perusal of other prospective buyers.

The first thing that must be considered before purchasing software is its compatibility with the computer on which it is to be used. If the program will not run efficiently on the computer in the classroom because of hardware limitations, there is no need to continue the evaluation process. Some of the restrictions to consider are the operating system (Windows or Macintosh) for which the particular software package was developed, the recommended memory size, the required hard drive space, the medium type (CD-ROM or DVD), the type of monitor, and the need for any special input devices such as a mouse or speech card. If a network is used in the classroom or school for which the program is to be purchased, it is also important to know if the program can be used on a network. Often, programs with many graphics encounter difficulties when accessed from a network.

There are three general steps to follow when evaluating a software program. First, one must read the instructions thoroughly to familiarize oneself with the program, its hardware requirements, and its installation. Second, once the program is installed and ready to run, the evaluator should first run the program as it would be run by a successful student, without deliberate errors but making use of all the possibilities available to the student. Third, the program should be run making deliberate mistakes to test the handling of errors. One should try to make as many different kinds of mistakes as possible, including those for incorrect keyboard usage and the validity of user directions.

Most software evaluation forms include the same types of information. There is usually a section for a general description of the program, consisting of the intended grade level, additional support materials available, the type of program (game, simulation, drill, etc.), stated goals and objectives, and the clarity of instructions. Other sections will provide checklists for educational content, presentation, and type and quality of user interaction with the program. Once a software package has been thoroughly tested, the teacher will be able to make an intelligent decision regarding its purchase.

When dealing with large class sizes and/or a limited number of computers available for student use, students can be rotated singly or in small groups to the computer centers—as long as they are well-oriented in advance to the task to be accomplished and the rules to be observed. Rules for using the computer should be reviewed with the whole class prior to individual computer usage and then prominently posted.

A computer lab is may be a good resource if it is available for use by the curriculum teacher, but the rules for the computer lab should be discussed before the class enters the lab. Students should have a thorough understanding of the assignment and of the consequences of disobeying the rules and/or damaging computer equipment. The teacher must be constantly on guard to prevent physical damage to the machines, such as from foreign objects finding their way into disk drives, key caps disappearing from keyboards (or being rearranged), or stray pencil or pen marks appearing on computer systems.

Students who have access to computers outside of school may feel like they already understand lab etiquette or program usage and thus ignore teacher instruction. Experienced students also may be more tempted than inexperienced students to save games on hard drives, move files into new directories or eliminate them altogether, create passwords to prevent others from using machines, and so on.

At the same time, other students may need assistance. It is possible to pair inexperienced students with more capable ones to alleviate some of these problems.

SKILL 12.2 Identify appropriate classroom procedures for student use of available technology

To a novice, computers might appear to be very complicated machines, but today's computers are user friendly. Once the computer is attached to the power source and turned on, most machines are configured to boot up into a menu of programs from which the user has merely to click on the desired choice.

For the computer to boot up from the hard drive according to its original configuration, it is necessary to remove any disks, CDs, or DVDs from the disk drive before turning on the power. Otherwise, the computer will not boot up into its menu from the hard drive, but rather will try to find the necessary boot up instructions on the disk.

When preparing to shut down the computer, it is important to close all programs that are currently in use. This includes saving anything that needs to be kept for future sessions on the computer. When a program is not properly exited, important data might be lost and the computer might not boot up to the proper menu the next time it is turned on. If the program was accessed from a DOS prompt or menu, the computer should be returned to the same starting place before turning off the machine. Programs accessed from Windows should be exited, all windows should be closed, and Windows itself should be exited before the power is turned off.

MacIntosh computers are much like Windows in that all programs should be exited and all windows closed before choosing SYSTEM and SHUT DOWN. Once everything is properly closed, the computer will alert the user and the computer can be turned off.

SKILL 12.3 Identify policies and procedures for the safe and ethical use of the Internet, networks, and other electronic media

Computer usage agreements define a number of criteria for the use of technology that students must agree to in order to have access to school computers. Students must exercise responsibility and accountability when using technology during the school day. Students who violate any parts of the computer usage agreement are subject to have all access to school computers or other educational technology denied or blocked, which, for the student needing to print a paper using the school computer and printer, could make the difference in handing assignments in on time or receiving a lower grade for late assignments.

District and school policies are developed to provide a consistent language of expectation for students using school technology. Districts are liable for the actions of students and teachers in school communities who use publicly funded and legislatively funded technology. The standards of usage for school computers are created to maximize student use for educational purposes and minimize student surfing for noneducational sites that distract during class times. The timeframes for school computer usage are limited for students because the numbers of computers available is limited.

Policies for technology use trickle down from the district to school communities to students and staff; federal and state funding to districts is conditional upon meeting certain safety guidelines. These policies and procedures for school usage are necessary to protect students from potentially dangerous situations when they are using computers for educational purposes.

Students who have their computer privileges revoked due to abuse of the Internet agreements may find that academic progress is jeopardized, especially if the students do not own computers or have Internet access beyond the classrooms.

Teachers should monitor the activities of students who are using computers and actively respond to students who misuse public technology intended to enhance the learning process and access for all students.

> *Beyond computer usage in schools, the use of other electronics such as iPods, portable gaming consoles, and cell phones are prohibited in most classrooms. These items can impede students from maintaining focus on the lesson objectives. An effective teacher underscores in the classroom that the focus on learning will be exclusive of electronic distractions and inappropriate computer use.*

SKILL 12.4 **Identify strategies for instructing students in the use of search techniques, the evaluation of data collected, and the preparation of presentations**

Technology and Research

The Internet and other research resources provide a wealth of information on thousands of interesting topics for students preparing presentations or projects. Using search engines, such as Google and Yahoo!, students can search multiple Internet resources on one subject search. Students should have an outline of the purpose of a project or research presentation that includes:

- Purpose: Identity the reason for the research and project.

- Objective: Having a clear thesis for a project will allow for specific Internet searches.

- Preparation: When using resources or collecting data, students should create folders for sorting through the information. Providing labels for the folders will create a system of organization that will make construction of the final project or presentation easier and less time consuming.

- Procedure: Organized folders and a procedural list of what the project or presentation needs to include will aid students in creating high-quality work.

- Visuals or artifacts: Choose data or visuals that are specific to the subject content or presentation. Make sure that poster boards or multimedia presentations can be seen from all areas of the classroom. Teachers can provide laptop computers for multimedia presentations.

When a teacher models and instructs students in the proper use of search techniques, the teacher can minimize wasted time in preparing projects and wasted paper from students who print every search. In some school districts, students are allowed a maximum number of printed pages per week. Since students have Internet accounts for computer usage, printing is easily monitored by the school's librarian and classroom teachers.

Having the school's librarian or technology expert as a guest speaker in classrooms provides another method of sharing and modeling proper presentation preparation using technology. Teachers can also appoint "technology experts" among students to work with others on projects and presentations. In high schools, technology classes provide students with upper class teacher assistants who fill the role of technology assistants.

The wealth of resources for teachers and students seeking to incorporate technology and structured planning for student presentations and projects is as diverse as the presentations. There is an expert in every classroom who is always willing to offer advice and instruction. In school communities, that expert may be the teacher.

Many school districts have networks that allow users to share files of lesson and unit plans, curriculum maps, pacing guides, and assessment ideas. While these can be very beneficial, it is always a good idea to determine the intended use for such files and documents before using them.

COMPETENCY 13
KNOWLEDGE OF THE HISTORY OF EDUCATION AND ITS PHILOSOPHICAL AND SOCIOLOGICAL FOUNDATIONS

SKILL 13.1 Apply historical, philosophical, and sociological perspectives to contemporary issues in American education

To understand where we are today in American public education is to appreciate how politics, history, research, society, and the economy have all come together to develop a complex system of teaching and learning.

Debates on instruction have typically focused on the role of the teacher. Some people argue that child-centered instruction is favorable, as it is more engaging for students. Others have advocated for more traditional methods, such as lecturing, note-taking, and other teacher-centered activities.

Historically, public education was relegated to the wealthy. Education was usually private, tutor-based, and uneven. The concept of a free public education was developed in order to ensure that many people in this country could participate in (and further develop) the nation's economy. Decades ago, a small one-room schoolhouse sufficed, but today, each neighborhood requires multiple schools to educate all of the local children.

As the population has grown, the structure of public schools has changed so that all children receive an equal education, no matter which school he attends. Simultaneously, new, more engaging instructional styles emerged; many classroom teachers began to incorporate cooperative learning, learning centers, reading and writing workshops, group projects, and other developmentally appropriate styles of teaching into their classrooms.

Another huge change in schools has been governance. GOVERNANCE refers to how schools are run. Even though schools are still technically run by local, elected school boards, the federal government is increasingly taking a role in public education. In the past, schools would have to answer to no higher authority than state government. Now, with the *No Child Left Behind Act*, the federal government has taken a more significant role in prescribing how schools are run.

GOVERNANCE: how schools are run

Another issue in governance has been the debate between local schools, neighborhood schools, and choice schools. Neighborhood schools are those which students attend based on their home address. For the past few decades, some school districts have provided students with the option of attending magnet schools, or schools that are available for any student within the district.

Usually, these schools have themes, such as business academies or college preparatory curricula. In addition to magnet schools, money is now available for charter schools that do not have to abide by the same policies as regular public schools. Magnet schools do not have to be run by school districts, but they take money from the districts in which their students originate. So, for example, if the local public school gets $5,000 per student per school year from local property taxes and the state (or however the state finances schools), that $5,000 would instead go to the charter school if one student opted to go there.

Finally, in some states and cities, voucher money is available for students attending private schools. This is where the government gives parents part or all of the money that would have been put into the local public district(s) so that they can use it to send their children to private schools. The pros and cons of all of these options are widely debated in the United States.

Philosophically, most of the debate that has shaped public education has focused on curriculum, instruction, and assessment. For example, standards-based education is a curricular move to ensure that all students from a state obtain the same knowledge. Debate has centered on three ideas: first, that some knowledge is not developmentally appropriate; second, that the standards are not appropriate for all students; third, that most states' standards are too thick, causing teachers to have to teach *too* much in a school year (and, therefore, not allowing teachers to go into depth with particular topics that may be of interest to students).

Debates on instruction have focused on the role of the teacher. Some people argue that child-centered instruction is favorable as it is more engaging for students. Others have advocated for more traditional methods, such as lecturing, note-taking, and other teacher-centered activities.

Debates on assessment have focused on the role of testing students, as well as the appropriateness of testing them for school evaluation purposes. First, most state tests take hours to complete, and many teachers argue that this wastes instructional time. Others argue that state tests do not assess what is really taught in schools.

Some educators suggest that performance assessments would be more appropriate. Performance assessments evaluate students' ability to do tasks related to their learning. For example, a performance assessment in language arts could be a timed essay. The teacher would score it with a rubric or scoring guide.

The best method for grading students has also been widely debated. Some teachers advocate eliminating letter grades; some school districts have even started to grade students not by subject, but by standard (taken from state standards).

Sociologically, schools have faced many challenges related to changes in demographics and economics within school districts. While laws have been set up to eliminate segregation in schools, many inner-city children attend highly segregated schools based on the demographic compositions of their neighborhoods.

For some time, districts instituted busing policies to combat this segregation. Busing means that a student in one neighborhood is put on a bus and sent to a school in another neighborhood with a different ethnic or racial composition. Many districts found that this was impractical, however, as it caused some students to have to spend hours per day on buses when they could have been doing other more productive things.

Many districts around the country are just learning how to accommodate larger immigrant populations as more immigrants enter through entry points that have not been historically popular. Those districts must learn how to develop appropriate English language programs to assist their students in learning English; they must also understand how to approach parents who may be hesitant to become involved with the school system.

SKILL 13.2 Identify contemporary philosophical views on education that influence teaching

All teachers are faced with the challenge of deciding whether they believe that the classroom should be run in a teacher-centered or student-centered fashion; for maximum student achievement, a combination of both is preferred.

Teacher-centered classrooms generally focus on the concept that knowledge is objective and that students must learn new information through the transmission of that knowledge from the teacher. Student-centered classrooms are considered to be constructivist, in that students are given opportunities to construct their own meanings to new pieces of knowledge. Doing so may require that students are more actively involved in the learning process. Indeed, constructivism is a strong force in teaching today, but it is often misinterpreted. Good constructivist teachers do not just let their students explore anything they want in any way they choose; rather, they give students opportunities to learn things in more instinctive and engaging ways, such as experiments, hands-on projects, class discussion, and so on.

For quite some time, a movement called multiple intelligences was popular in many classrooms. This theory suggested that there are at least seven different types of intelligence, and that verbal and quantitative intelligences—the two types that are most often associated with intellect—should be reconsidered as less important as they once were. Other intelligences included kinesthetic, interpersonal, musical, intrapersonal, and spatial. This theory helped teachers understand that while some students may not be comfortable with one style of learning, it is entirely possible that they excel in another.

Various subject areas have complicated philosophical debates of teaching. For example, reading teachers have long debated whether phonics or whole language was more appropriate as an instructional methodology. Language arts teachers have debated the importance of the canon (famous works of literature); some teachers feel that the canon is irrelevant and that the only reason to teach literature is to teach thinking skills and an appreciation of good literature. Math teachers have debated the extent to which application is necessary in math instruction; some feel that it is more important to teach structure and process, while others feel it is only important to teach math skills in context.

COMPETENCY 14

KNOWLEDGE OF SPECIFIC APPROACHES, METHODS, AND STRATEGIES APPROPRIATE FOR STUDENTS WITH LIMITED ENGLISH PROFICIENCY

SKILL 14.1 Identify characteristics of first and second language acquisition

> *One of the most important things to know about the differences between first language (L1) and second language (L2) acquisition is that people usually will master L1, but they will almost never be fully proficient in L2.*

One of the most important things to know about the differences between first language (L1) and second language (L2) acquisition is that people usually will master L1, but they will almost never be fully proficient in L2. However, if children can be immersed in L2 before about the age of seven, their chances at full mastery will be much higher.

Children learn language with little effort, which is why they can babble at one year and speak with complete, complex ideas just a few years later. It is important to know that language is innate, meaning that our brains are ready to learn a language from birth. Yet a lot of language learning is behavioral, meaning that children imitate adults' speech.

L2 acquisition is much harder for adults. One of the more notable theories of L2 acquisition comes from Jim Cummins. Cummins argues that there are two types of language that usually need to be acquired by students learning English as a second language: basic interpersonal communication skills (BICS) and cognitive academic language proficiency (CALP).

BICS is general, everyday language used to communicate simple thoughts, whereas CALP is the more complex, academic language used in school. It is harder for students to acquire CALP, and many teachers mistakenly assume that students can learn complex academic concepts in English if they have already mastered BICS. The truth is that CALP takes much longer to master, and in some cases, particularly with little exposure in certain subjects, it may never be mastered.

Another set of theories is based on Stephen Krashen's research in L2 acquisition. Most people understand his theories based on five principles:

1. The acquisition-learning hypothesis: This states that there is a difference between learning a language and acquiring it. Children "acquire" a first language easily—it's natural. But adults often have to "learn" a language

through coursework, studying, and memorizing. One can acquire a second language, but often it requires more deliberate and natural interaction within that language.

2. The monitor hypothesis: This is when the learned language "monitors" the acquired language. In other words, this is when a person's "grammar check" kicks in and keeps awkward, incorrect language out of L2 communication.

3. The natural order hypothesis: This suggests that the learning of grammatical structures is predictable and follows a "natural order."

4. The input hypothesis: Some people call this "comprehensible input." This means that a language learner will learn best when the instruction or conversation is just above the learner's ability. That way, the learner has the foundation to understand most of the language, but still will have to figure out, often in context, what that extra, more difficult, element means.

5. The affective filter hypothesis: This suggests that people will learn a second language when they are relaxed, have high levels of motivation, and have a decent level of self-confidence.

English for speakers of other language (ESOL) students may need additional accommodations with assessments, assignments, and projects. For example, teachers may find that written tests provide little to no information about a student's understanding of the content. Therefore, an oral test may be better suited for ESOL students. When students are somewhat comfortable and capable with written tests, a shortened test may actually be preferable; take note that they will need extra time to translate.

SKILL 14.2 Identify ESOL approaches, methods, and strategies (e.g., materials adaptation, alternative assessment, and strategy documentation) appropriate for instruction

Teaching students who are learning English as a second language poses some unique challenges, particularly in a standards-based environment. The key is realizing that no matter how little English a student knows, the teacher should teach with the student's developmental level in mind. This means that instruction should not be "dumbed-down" for ESOL students. Different approaches should be used, however, to ensure that these students get multiple opportunities to learn and practice English and still learn content.

Many ESOL approaches are based on social learning methods. When placed in mixed-level groups or paired with a student of another ability level, students will get a chance to practice English in a natural, nonthreatening environment. Students should not be pushed in these groups to use complex language or to experiment with words that are too difficult. They should simply get a chance to practice with simple words and phrases.

In teacher-directed instructional situations, visual aids such as pictures, objects, and video are particularly effective at helping students make connections between words and items with which they are already familiar.

> ### SKILL 14.3 Identify and apply cognitive approaches, multisensory ESOL strategies, and instructional practices that build upon students' abilities and promote self-worth

Approaches to Teaching L2

A common method for learning a language often involves drills, memorization, and tests (alternately referred to as a structural, grammatical, or linguistic approach). While this works for some students, it certainly does not work for all.

Although dozens of methods have been developed to help people learn additional languages, a few are the most common approaches used in today's K–12 classrooms. One such method is the cognitive approach to language learning, which focuses on concepts. When teachers use the cognitive approach, they focus on using language for conceptual purposes, rather than learning words and grammar for the sake of simply learning new words and grammatical structures. This approach focuses heavily on students' learning styles, and it cannot necessarily be pinned down as having specific techniques. Rather, it is more of a philosophy of instruction.

In a general sense, when teachers work to motivate students to learn a language, they do things to help reduce fear and to help students identify with native speakers of the target language. A very common method is often called the functional approach. In this approach, the teacher focuses on communicative elements. For example, a first-grade ESOL teacher might help students learn phrases that will assist them in finding a restroom, asking for help on the playground, and other everyday scenarios.

Another very common motivational approach is total physical response. This is a kinesthetic approach that combines language learning and physical movement. In essence, students learn new vocabulary and grammar by responding with physical motion to verbal commands. Some people say it is particularly effective because the physical actions help to create solid mental connections with the words.

Other Language Learning Considerations

In addition to these methods, it is important that teachers communicate and collaborate in order to provide a certain amount of consistency in language instruction—particularly when second language learners have multiple teachers, such as in middle or high school. It is particularly difficult for second language learners to go from one class to the next, where there are different sets of expectations and varied methods of instruction, and still focus on the more complex elements of learning language.

When students have higher levels of anxiety regarding the learning of a second language, they will be less likely to focus on the language; rather, they will be focusing on whatever it is that is creating their anxiety. This does not mean that standards and expectations should be different for these students in all classes; it simply means that teachers should have common expectations so that students feel prepared in each class and don't become distracted by differing expectations.

Another hugely important reason for teachers to collaborate, particularly with the ESOL specialists, is to ensure that students are showing consistent development across classes. Where there is inconsistency, teachers should work to uncover what is keeping the student from excelling in a particular class.

Perhaps the most important consideration regarding the difference between learning a first language versus a second one is that if the learner is approximately age seven or older, learning a second language will occur very differently in the learner's brain than it would have if the learner had been younger.

The reason for this is that there is a language-learning function that exists in young children that appears to go away as they mature. The ability to learn a language prior to age seven is almost guaranteed, requiring relatively little effort. Some theorists, including the famous linguist Noam Chomsky, argue that the brain has a "universal grammar," and thus only vocabulary and particular grammatical structures related to a specific language need to be introduced in order for a child to learn it. However, this is definitely not the case with learning a second language after about seven years old.

Learning a second language as a preadolescent, an adolescent, or an adult requires quite a bit of translation from the first language to the second. Vocabulary and grammar particulars are memorized, not necessarily internalized (at least, not as readily as a first language). In fact, many (though not all) people who are immersed in a second language are never fully fluent in the language.

> In general, the best language-teaching methods do not treat students as if they have a language deficit. Rather, the best methods build upon what students already know, and they help to instill the target language as a communicative process rather than a list of vocabulary words that have to be memorized.

It is fairly clear that learning a second language successfully first requires fluency in the speaker's native language. This is because, as stated above, the second language is translated from the first in the learner's mind. First language literacy is also a crucial factor in second language learning, particularly for second language literacy.

When helping second language learners make the crossover in language fluency or literacy from the first language to the second language, it is important to help them identify strategies that they use in the first language and apply those to the second language. It is also important to note similarities and differences in phonetic principals in the two languages. Sometimes it is helpful to encourage students to translate; other times, it is helpful for them to practice production in the target language. In either case, teachers must realize that learning a second language is a slow and complicated process.

SAMPLE TEST

SAMPLE TEST

(Average) (Skill 1.1)

1. **What would improve planning for instruction?**

    A. Describe the role of the teacher and student

    B. Evaluate the outcomes of instruction

    C. Rearrange the order of activities

    D. Give outside assignments

(Rigorous) (Skill 1.1)

2. **What is the best definition for an achievement test?**

    A. It measures mechanical and practical abilities

    B. It measures broad areas of knowledge that are the result of cumulative learning experiences

    C. It measures the ability to learn to perform a task

    D. It measures performance related to specific, recently acquired information

(Rigorous) (Skill 1.1)

3. **Norm-referenced tests:**

    A. Give information only about the local samples results

    B. Provide information about how the local test takers did compared to a representative sampling of national test takers

    C. Make no comparisons to national test takers

    D. None of the above

(Easy) (Skill 1.1)

4. **A standardized test may be:**

    A. Given out with the same predetermined questions and format to all

    B. Given to certain children, but not all

    C. Taken over a lengthier test period if given out in exactly the same format with the same content

    D. All of the above

(Rigorous) (Skill 1.2)

5. **Which of the following describes why it is important and necessary for teachers to be able to analyze data on their students?**

    A. So that they can provide appropriate instruction

    B. So that they can make instructional decisions

    C. So that they can communicate and determine instructional progress

    D. All of the above

(Average) (Skill 1.2)

6. **How are standardized tests useful in assessment?**

    A. For teacher evaluation

    B. For evaluation of the administration

    C. For comparison from school to school

    D. For comparison to the population on which the test was normed

(Average) (Skill 1.3)

7. **What is evaluation of instructional activity based on?**

    A. Student grades

    B. Teacher evaluation

    C. Student participation

    D. Specified criteria

(Average) (Skill 1.3)

8. **What must be a consideration when a parent complains that he or she cannot control his or her child's behavior?**

    A. Whether the parent gives feedback to the child

    B. Whether the parent's expectations for control are developmentally appropriate

    C. How much time the parent spends with the child

    D. How rigid the rules are that the parent sets

(Rigorous) (Skill 1.3)

9. **If teachers attend to content, instructional materials, activities, learner needs, and goals in instructional planning, what could be an outcome?**

    A. Planning for the next year

    B. Effective classroom performance

    C. Elevated test scores on standardized tests

    D. More student involvement

(Rigorous) (Skill 1.4)

10. **Mrs. Grant provides her students with many extrinsic motivators in order to increase their intrinsic motivation. Which of the following best explains this relationship?**

    A. This is a good relationship, and it will increase intrinsic motivation

    B. This relationship builds animosity between the teacher and the students

    C. Extrinsic motivation alone does not help to build intrinsic motivation

    D. There is no place for extrinsic motivation in the classroom

(Easy) (Skill 1.4)

11. **Which of the following is considered a study skill?**

    A. Using graphs, tables, and maps

    B. Using a desktop publishing program

    C. Explaining important vocabulary words

    D. Asking for clarification

(Easy) (Skill 1.4)

12. **Which of the following test items is not objective?**

    A. Multiple choice

    B. Essay

    C. Matching

    D. True/false

(Rigorous) (Skill 2.1)

13. **What should a teacher do when students do not respond well to an instructional activity?**

    A. Reevaluate learner needs

    B. Request administrative help

    C. Continue with the activity another day

    D. Assign homework on the concept

(Average) (Skill 2.1)

14. **Why is it important for a teacher to pose a question before calling on students to answer?**

    A. It helps manage student conduct

    B. It keeps the students as a group focused on the class work

    C. It allows students time to collaborate

    D. It gives the teacher time to walk among the students

(Average) (Skill 2.1)

15. **Which statement is an example of specific praise?**

    A. "John, you are the only person in class not paying attention."

    B. "William, I thought we agreed that you would turn in all of your homework."

    C. "Robert, you did a good job staying in line. See how it helped us get to music class on time?"

    D. "Class, you did a great job cleaning up the art room."

(Easy) (Skill 2.1)

16. **What is one way a teacher can supplement verbal praise?**

    A. Help students evaluate their own performance and supply self-reinforcement

    B. Give verbal praise more frequently

    C. Give tangible rewards such as stickers or treats

    D. Have students practice giving verbal praise

(Average) (Skill 2.1)

17. **The teacher states that students will review the material from the previous day, demonstrate an electronic circuit, and set up an electronic circuit in small groups. What has the teacher demonstrated?**

    A. The importance of reviewing

    B. Giving the general framework for the lesson to facilitate learning

    C. Giving students the opportunity to leave if they are not interested in the lesson

    D. Providing momentum for the lesson

(Average) (Skill 2.1)

18. **What is one benefit of amplifying a student's response?**

    A. It helps the student develop a positive self-image

    B. It is helpful to other students who are in the process of learning the reasoning or steps in answering the question

    C. It allows the teacher to cover more content

    D. It helps to keep the information organized

(Average) (Skill 2.1)

19. **How can the teacher help students become more work-oriented and less disruptive?**

    A. Seek their input for content instruction

    B. Challenge the students with a task and show genuine enthusiasm for it

    C. Use behavior modification techniques with all students

    D. Make sure lesson plans are complete for the week

(Rigorous) (Skill 2.1)

20. **What is an established method for increasing student originality, intrinsic motivation, and higher-order thinking skills?**

    A. Painting the walls a neutral color

    B. Setting high expectations

    C. Providing student choice

    D. Use of authentic learning opportunities

(Rigorous) (Skill 2.1)

21. **Why is it important for the teacher to alert nonperformers when conducting activities?**

    A. It creates suspense

    B. Students will take over the discipline

    C. Students will become more work involved

    D. Students will more likely not take part in the recitation

(Rigorous) (Skill 2.1)

22. **Ms. Smith says, "Exactly what do you mean by, 'It was the author's intention to mislead you'?" What does this illustrate?**

    A. Digression

    B. Restating a response

    C. Probing a response

    D. Amplifying a response

(Rigorous) (Skill 2.1)

23. **What is a frequently used type of feedback to students?**

    A. Correctives

    B. Confirmation

    C. Correcting the response

    D. Explanations

(Rigorous) (Skill 2.1)

24. **What is the definition of a nonperformer?**

    A. Students who are off-task

    B. Students not chosen to answer a teacher-posed question

    C. Students with stanine scores of 20 or below

    D. Students who consistently score below 50 percent on classroom tests

(Rigorous) (Skill 2.1)

25. **What is *not* a way that teachers show acceptance and give value to a student response?**

    A. Acknowledging

    B. Correcting

    C. Discussing

    D. Amplifying

(Rigorous) (Skill 2.1)

26. **What is teacher with-it-ness?**

    A. Having adequate knowledge of subject matter

    B. A skill that must be mastered to attain certification

    C. Understanding the current fads and trends that affect students

    D. When a teacher gives a sense that she knows what she is doing

(Rigorous) (Skill 2.1)

27. **The teacher responds, "Yes, that is correct" to a student's answer. What is this an example of?**

    A. Academic feedback

    B. Academic praise

    C. Simple positive response

    D. Simple negative response

(Average) (Skill 2.1)

28. **What are teacher redirects?**

    A. When the teacher redirects deviant behavior to another task

    B. When the teacher changes the focus of the class to provide smooth transitions

    C. When the teacher changes student jobs every nine weeks

    D. When the teacher asks a second student to expound on the first student's answer

(Rigorous) (Skill 2.2)

29. **When is the optimal benefit reached when handling an incorrect student response?**

    A. When graded work is returned to the student

    B. When the other students are allowed to correct that student

    C. When the student understands how to use the feedback

    D. When the teacher asks simple questions, provides cues to clarify, or gives assistance for working out the correct response

(Average) (Skill 2.3)

30. **The effective teacher communicates nonverbally with students by:**

    A. Writing directions on the board

    B. Using facial expressions to express dissatisfaction instead of correcting the student verbally

    C. Using positive body language and expressing warmth, concern, and acceptance

    D. Not making eye contact with students

(Rigorous) (Skill 2.3)

31. **Efficient use of time includes which of the following?**

    A. Daily review, seatwork, and recitation of concepts

    B. Lesson initiation, transition, and comprehension check

    C. Review, test, review

    D. Punctuality and management transition

(Rigorous) (Skill 2.3)

32. **In a success-oriented classroom, mistakes are viewed as:**

    A. Motivations to improve

    B. A natural part of the learning process

    C. Ways to improve

    D. Building blocks

(Easy) (Skill 2.3)

33. **Which of the following can affect the desire of students to learn new material?**

    A. Assessment plans

    B. Lesson plans

    C. Enthusiasm

    D. School community

(Easy) (Skill 2.3)

34. **A teacher's posture and movement affect the following student outcomes *except*:**

    A. Student learning

    B. Attitudes

    C. Motivation

    D. Physical development

(Rigorous) (Skill 2.3)

35. **What is proactive classroom management?**

    A. Management that is constantly changing

    B. Management that is downplayed

    C. Management that gives clear and explicit instructions and rewarding compliance

    D. Management that is designed by the students

(Average) (Skill 2.4)

36. **What is the most significant development emerging in children at age two?**

    A. Immune system develops

    B. Socialization occurs

    C. Language develops

    D. Perception develops

(Easy) (Skill 2.4)

37. **When communicating with parents for whom English is not the primary language, you should:**

    A. Provide materials whenever possible in their native language

    B. Use an interpreter

    C. Provide the same communication as you would to native English-speaking parents

    D. All of the above

(Average) (Skill 2.4)

38. **What has research shown to be the effect of using advance organizers in the lesson?**

    A. They facilitate learning and retention

    B. They enhance retention only

    C. They only serve to help the teacher organize the lesson

    D. They show definitive positive results on student achievement

(Average) (Skill 3.1)

39. **In promoting professional development opportunities for teachers that enhance student achievement, the following must be considered:**

    A. Teachers must be provided time to complete the training at minimal cost

    B. Teachers must use data to choose training that correlates with areas of student needs

    C. Teachers must complete required training hours to maintain their teacher certification

    D. All of the above

(Rigorous) (Skill 3.1)

40. **In reviewing FCAT reading scores for his current students, Mr. Garcia finds that 40 percent of his students failed to meet standards on main idea and purpose. Which of the following professional development activities should Mr. Garcia choose to improve achievement for his current students?**

    A. Comprehension reading strategies

    B. Vocabulary development

    C. Behavior management

    D. FCAT test preparation

(Rigorous) (Skill 3.2)

41. Mr. Graham has taken the time to reflect, complete observations, and ask for feedback about the interactions between him and his students from his principal. It is obvious by seeking this information out that Mr. Graham understands which of the following?

    A. The importance of clear communication with the principal

    B. That he needs to analyze the effectiveness of his classroom interactions

    C. That he is clearly communicating with the principal

    D. That he cares about his students

(Easy) (Skill 3.2)

42. Which of the following is a good reason to collaborate with a peer?

    A. To increase your knowledge in areas where you feel you are weak, but the peer is strong

    B. To increase your planning time and that of your peer by combining the classes and taking more breaks

    C. To have fewer lesson plans to write

    D. To teach fewer subjects

(Rigorous) (Skill 3.2)

43. Which of the following are ways a professional can assess his or her teaching strengths and weaknesses?

    A. Examining how many students are unable to understand a concept

    B. Asking peers for suggestions or ideas

    C. Self-evaluation/reflection of lessons taught

    D. All of the above

(Average) (Skill 4.1)

44. Which of the following might improve planning for instruction?

    A. Describing the role of the teacher and student

    B. Evaluating the outcomes of instruction

    C. Rearranging the order of activities

    D. Giving outside assignments

(Rigorous) (Skill 4.1)

45. The professional teacher provides realistic projects and problem solving activities that will enable all students to demonstrate their ability to think creatively. Which of the following is an example of a project that will develop critical thinking?

    A. Ask students to list items they would purchase from a catalog

    B. Ask students to determine total cost of order from the catalog

    C. Ask students to find another source for purchasing the items

    D. Ask students to compare shopping ads or catalog deals

(Average) (Skill 4.1)

46. Which of the following is *not* one of the levels of Bloom's taxonomy?

    A. Synthesis

    B. Evaluation

    C. Understanding

    D. Knowledge

(Rigorous) (Skill 4.1)

47. Mr. Ryan has proposed to his classroom that the students may demonstrate understanding of the unit taught in a variety of ways, including taking a test, writing a paper, creating an oral presentation, or building a model/project. Which of the following areas of differentiation has Mr. Ryan demonstrated?

  A. Synthesis

  B. Product

  C. Content

  D. Process

(Average) (Skill 4.1)

48. What is an example of a low-order question?

  A. Why is it important to recycle items in your home?

  B. Compare how glass and plastics are recycled.

  C. What items do we recycle in our county?

  D. Explain the importance of recycling in our county.

(Easy) (Skill 4.1)

49. What is the most important benefit of students developing critical thinking skills?

  A. Students are able to apply knowledge to a specific subject area as well as other subject areas

  B. Students remember the information for testing purposes

  C. Students focus on a limited number of specific facts

  D. Students do not have to memorize the information for later recall

(Average) (Skill 4.1)

50. When is content teaching effective?

  A. When it is presented in demonstration form

  B. When the teacher separates the content into distinct elements

  C. When the content is covered over a long span of time

  D. When the decision about content is made at the district level

(Average) (Skill 4.2)

51. Wait-time has what effect?

  A. Gives structure to the class discourse

  B. Fewer chain and low-level questions are asked with more higher-level questions included

  C. Gives the students time to evaluate the response

  D. Gives the opportunity for in-depth discussion about the topic

(Rigorous) (Skill 4.2)

52. Teachers who want to improve creative thinking in their students can use which of the following strategies?

  A. Increase wait time to 5 seconds

  B. Ask deliberate questions

  C. Ask students to journal and reflect on what they just learned

  D. All of the above

(Average) (Skill 5.1)

53. How can the teacher establish a positive climate in the classroom?

   A. Help students see the positive aspects of various cultures

   B. Use whole group instruction for all content areas

   C. Help students divide into cooperative groups based on ability

   D. Eliminate teaching strategies that allow students to make choices

(Average) (Skill 5.1)

54. What do cooperative learning methods all have in common?

   A. Multiple intelligence philosophy

   B. Cooperative task/cooperative reward structures

   C. Student roles and communication

   D. Teacher-centered roles

(Average) (Skill 5.2)

55. What is a good strategy for teaching a group of ethnically diverse students?

   A. Don't focus on the students' culture

   B. Expect them to assimilate easily into your classroom

   C. Imitate their speech patterns

   D. Include ethnic studies in the curriculum

(Rigorous) (Skill 6.1)

56. What developmental patterns should a professional teacher assess to meet the needs of the student?

   A. Academic, regional, and family background

   B. Social, physical, and academic

   C. Academic, physical, and family background

   D. Physical, family, and ethnic background

(Average) (Skill 6.2)

57. According to the Principles of Professional Conduct for the Education Profession in Florida, an individual educator's certificate can be revoked or suspended if the following happens:

   A. Teacher is accused of hurting a child

   B. Teacher fails to self-report within forty-eight (48) hours to appropriate authorities (as determined by district) any arrests/charges involving the abuse of a child

   C. Teacher uses curse words in front of a parent

   D. Teacher fails to attend mandatory training

(Easy) (Skill 6.2)

58. Teachers must hold themselves to high standards. When they engage in negative actions such as fighting with students, they are violating all of the following except:

   A. Ethics

   B. Professionalism

   C. Morals

   D. Fiscal

(Average) (Skill 7.1)

59. **Students who can solve problems mentally have:**

    A. Reached maturity

    B. Physically developed

    C. Reached the preoperational stage of thought

    D. Achieved the ability to manipulate objects symbolically

(Easy) (Skill 7.1)

60. **Mrs. Potts is in the middle of her math lesson, but notices that many of her students seem to be having some sort of difficulty. Mrs. Potts stops class and decides to have a class meeting. Although her math objectives are important, it is equally important to address whatever is troubling her classroom. This is because:**

    A. Discipline is important

    B. Social issues can impact academic learning

    C. Maintaining order is important

    D. Social skills instruction is important

(Average) (Skill 7.1)

61. **When seeking the successful inclusion of students with disabilities:**

    A. A variety of instructional arrangements are available

    B. School personnel shift the responsibility for learning outcomes to the student

    C. The physical facilities are used as they are

    D. Regular classroom teachers have sole responsibility for evaluating student progress

(Average) (Skill 7.2)

62. **Which of the following is not a communication issue that is related to diversity within the classroom?**

    A. Learning disorder

    B. Sensitive terminology

    C. Body language

    D. Discussing differing viewpoints and opinions

(Rigorous) (Skill 7.3)

63. **When are students more likely to understand complex ideas?**

    A. If they do outside research before coming to class

    B. When they write out the definitions of complex words

    C. When they attend a lecture on the subject

    D. When the ideas are clearly defined by the teacher and students are given examples and nonexamples of the concept

(Rigorous) (Skill 7.3)

64. **What have recent studies regarding effective teachers concluded?**

    A. Effective teachers let students establish rules

    B. Effective teachers establish routines by the sixth week of school

    C. Effective teachers state their own policies and establish consistent class rules and procedures on the first day of class

    D. Effective teachers establish flexible routines

(Average) (Skill 7.3)

65. When is utilization of instructional materials most effective?

   A. When the activities are sequenced

   B. When the materials are prepared ahead of time

   C. When the students choose the pages to work on

   D. When the students create the instructional materials

(Easy) (Skill 7.3)

66. If teachers attend to content, instructional materials, activities, learner needs, and goals in instructional planning, what could be an outcome?

   A. Planning for the next year

   B. Effective classroom performance

   C. Elevated test scores on standardized tests

   D. More student involvement

(Average) (Skill 7.3)

67. When creating and selecting materials for instruction, teachers should complete which of the following steps:

   A. Ensure material is relevant to the prior knowledge of the students

   B. Allow for a variation of learning styles

   C. Choose alternative teaching strategies

   D. All of the above

(Rigorous) (Skill 7.3)

68. The teacher states, "We will work on the first page of vocabulary words. On the second page we will work on the structure and meaning of the words. We will go over these together and then you will write out the answers to the exercises on your own. I will be circulating to give help if needed." What is this an example of?

   A. Evaluation of instructional activity

   B. Analysis of instructional activity

   C. Identification of expected outcomes

   D. Pacing of instructional activity

(Average) (Skill 7.4)

69. Which of the following is not a stage in Piaget's theory of child development?

   A. Sensory motor stage

   B. Preoptimal stage

   C. Concrete operational

   D. Formal operational

(Easy) (Skill 7.4)

70. Constructivist classrooms are considered to be:

   A. Student-centered

   B. Teacher-centered

   C. Focused on standardized tests

   D. Requiring little creativity

(Rigorous) (Skill 7.4)

71. **Mr. Rogers describes his educational philosophy as eclectic, meaning that he uses many educational theories to guide his classroom practice. Why is this the best approach for today's teachers?**

    A. Today's classrooms are often too diverse for one theory to meet the needs of all students

    B. Educators must be able to draw upon other strategies if one theory is not effective

    C. Both A and B

    D. None of the above

(Easy) (Skill 7.4)

72. **How many stages of intellectual development does Piaget define?**

    A. Two

    B. Four

    C. Six

    D. Eight

(Easy) (Skill 7.4)

73. **Who developed the theory of multiple intelligences?**

    A. Bruner

    B. Gardner

    C. Kagan

    D. Cooper

(Easy) (Skill 7.5)

74. **Which of the following is a presentation modification?**

    A. Taking an assessment in an alternate room

    B. Providing an interpreter to give the test in American Sign Language

    C. Allowing dictation of written responses

    D. Extending the time limits on an assessment

(Average) (Skill 7.5)

75. **Free appropriate education, the individual education program, procedural safeguards, and least restrictive environment; identify the legislation represented by these elements.**

    A. American with Disabilities Act

    B. The Equal Access Act

    C. The Individuals with Disabilities Education Act

    D. Title VI, The Civil Rights Act of 1964

(Average) (Skill 8.1)

76. **Mr. Sanchez is having his students work with one-syllable words, removing the first consonant and substituting another, as in changing mats to hats. What reading skill are they working on?**

    A. Morphemic inflections

    B. Pronouncing short vowels

    C. Invented spelling

    D. Phonemic awareness

(Average) (Skill 8.1)

77. Ms. James is seated with a child by her side. The child is reading aloud from an open book. Ms. James is teaching in a school that has embraced the balanced literacy approach. Therefore it is most likely that Ms. James is recording:

    A. The child's use of expression in reading aloud

    B. The child's errors and miscues

    C. Her observations of the child's attitude toward reading

    D. The child's feelings about the particular passage being read

(Easy) (Skill 8.2)

78. **In order to get children to understand specialized vocabulary, they can use:**

    A. Newspapers

    B. Internet resources and approved Web sites that focus on their special interest

    C. Experts they can interview

    D. All of the above

(Average) (Skills 8.3)

79. **When a student uses sticky notes to make comments or ask questions while reading a book, they are using the following reading comprehension strategy:**

    A. Text structure

    B. Graphic organizer

    C. Textual marking

    D. Summarization

(Easy) (Skill 8.4)

80. **Which of the following is an example of a synthesis question according to Bloom's taxonomy?**

    A. What is the definition of_____?

    B. Compare _____ to _____.

    C. Match column A to column B.

    D. Propose an alternative to_____

(Easy) (Skill 8.5)

81. **How can DVDs be used in instruction?**

    A. Students can use DVDs to create pictures for reports

    B. Students can use DVDs to create a science experiment

    C. Students can use DVDs to record class activities

    D. Students can use DVDs to review concepts studied

(Easy) (Skill 9.1)

82. **What might be a result if the teacher is distracted by some unrelated event in the instruction?**

    A. Students will leave the class

    B. Students will understand the importance of class rules

    C. Students will stay on-task longer

    D. Students will lose the momentum of the lesson

(Average) (Skill 9.2)

83. **How can student misconduct be redirected?**

   A. The teacher threatens the students with extra homework

   B. The teacher assigns detention to the whole class

   C. The teacher stops the activity and stares at the students

   D. The teacher effectively handles changing from one activity to another

(Rigorous) (Skill 9.2)

84. **Marcus is a first grade boy of good developmental attainment. His learning progress is good in the first half of the year. He shows no indicators of emotional distress. After the holiday break, he returns much changed. He is quieter, sullen even, tending to play alone. He has moments of tearfulness, sometimes almost without cause. He avoids contact with adults as often as he can. Even play with his friends has become limited. He has episodes of wetting not seen before and often wants to sleep in school. What approach is appropriate for this sudden change in behavior?**

   A. Give him some time to adjust after the holiday break

   B. Report this change immediately to administration; do not call the parents until administration decides a course of action

   C. Document his daily behavior carefully as soon as you notice such a change; report to administration in the next month or so in a meeting

   D. Make a courtesy call to the parents to let them know he is not acting like himself

(Average) (Skill 9.2)

85. **What is a sample of an academic transition signal?**

   A. How do clouds form?

   B. Today we are going to study clouds.

   C. We have completed today's lesson.

   D. That completes the description of cumulus clouds. Now we will look at the description of cirrus clouds.

(Average) (Skill 9.3)

86. **What should the teacher do when a student is tapping a pencil on the desk during a lecture?**

   A. Stop the lesson and correct the student as an example to other students

   B. Walk over to the student and quietly touch the pencil as a signal for the student to stop

   C. Announce to the class that everyone should remember to remain quiet during the lecture

   D. Ignore the student, hoping he or she will stop

(Rigorous) (Skill 9.3)

87. **What is one way of effectively managing student conduct?**

   A. State expectations about behavior

   B. Let students discipline their peers

   C. Let minor infractions of the rules go unnoticed

   D. Increase disapproving remarks

(Rigorous) (Skill 9.3)

88. **Why is punishment not always effective in managing student behavior?**

    A. It tends to suppress behavior, not eliminate it

    B. It focuses on the negative, rather than the positive

    C. Students may comply out of fear rather than a genuine behavior change

    D. All of the above

(Average) (Skill 9.3)

89. **Robert throws a piece of paper across the room. The teacher ignores Robert. What is the teacher demonstrating?**

    A. Punishment

    B. Extinction

    C. Negative practice

    D. Verbal reprimand

(Average) (Skill 9.3)

90. **To maintain the flow of events in the classroom, what should an effective teacher do?**

    A. Work only in small groups

    B. Use only whole class activities

    C. Direct attention to content, rather than focusing the class on misbehavior

    D. Follow lectures with written assignments

(Rigorous) (Skill 9.3)

91. **What is most likely to happen when students witness a punitive or angry desist?**

    A. Respond with more behavior disruption

    B. All disruptive behavior stops

    C. Students align with teacher

    D. Behavior stays the same

(Easy) (Skill 9.3)

92. **What can be measured utilizing the following types of assessments: direct observation, role playing, context observation, and teacher ratings?**

    A. Social skills

    B. Reading skills

    C. Math skills

    D. Need for specialized instruction

(Rigorous) (Skill 9.3)

93. **What increases the likelihood that the response following an event will occur again?**

    A. Extinction

    B. Satiation

    C. Verbal reprimands

    D. Reinforcement

(Average) (Skill 9.3)

94. **Why is praise for compliance important in classroom management?**

    A. Students will continue deviant behavior

    B. Desirable conduct will be repeated

    C. It reflects simplicity and warmth

    D. Students will fulfill obligations

(Rigorous) (Skill 10.1)

95. **When planning instruction, which of the following is an organizational tool to help ensure that you are providing a well-balanced set of objectives?**

    A. Using a taxonomy to develop objectives

    B. Determining prior knowledge skill levels

    C. Determining readiness levels

    D. Ensuring that you meet the needs of diverse learners

(Easy) (Skill 10.3)

96. **What should be considered when evaluating textbooks for content?**

    A. Type of print used

    B. Number of photos used

    C. Whether it is free of cultural stereotyping

    D. Outlines at the beginning of each chapter

(Average) (Skill 11.1)

97. **Which of the following could be an example of a situation that could have an effect on a student's learning and academic progress?**

    A. Relocation

    B. Abuse

    C. Both of the above

    D. Neither of the above

(Average) (Skill 11.1)

98. **Andy shows up to class acting aggressively and irritably. He is often late, sleeps in class, sometimes slurs his speech, and has an odor of alcohol. What is the first intervention to take?**

    A. Confront him, relying on a trusting relationship you think you have

    B. Do a lesson on alcohol abuse, making an example of him

    C. Do nothing, as it is better to err on the side of failing to identify substance abuse

    D. Call administration, avoid conflict, and supervise others carefully

(Average) (Skill 11.1)

99. **A sixteen-year-old girl who has been looking sad writes an essay in which the main protagonist commits suicide. You overhear her talking about suicide. What do you do?**

    A. Report this immediately to school administration and talk to the girl, letting her know you will talk to her parents about it

    B. Report this immediately to authorities

    C. Report this immediately to school administration or make your own report to authorities if required by protocol in your school and do nothing else

    D. Just give the child some extra attention, as it may just be that that is all she's looking for

(Rigorous) (Skill 11.1)

100. You are leading a substance abuse discussion for health class. The students present their belief that marijuana is not harmful to their health. What set of data would refute their claim?

A. It is more carcinogenic than nicotine, lowers resistance to infection, worsens acne, and damages brain cells

B. It damages brain cells, causes behavior changes in prenatally exposed infants, leads to other drug abuse, and causes short-term memory loss

C. It lowers tolerance for frustration, causes eye damage, increases paranoia, and lowers resistance to infection

D. It leads to abusing alcohol, lowers white blood cell count, reduces fertility, and causes gout

(Average) (Skill 11.1)

101. Jeanne, a bright, attentive student, is in first hour class, English. She is quiet, but very alert, often visually scanning the room in random patterns. Her pupils are dilated and she has a slight but noticeable tremor in her hands. She fails to note a cue given from her teacher. At odd moments she will act as if responding to stimuli that aren't there by suddenly changing her gaze. When spoken to directly, she has a limited response, but her teacher has a sense she is not herself. What should the teacher do?

A. Ask the student if she is all right, then let it go as there are not enough signals to be alarmed

B. Meet with the student after class to get more information before making a referral

C. Send the student to the office to see the health nurse

D. Quietly call for administration, remain calm, and be careful not to alarm the class

(Easy) (Skill 11.1)

102. A parent has left an angry message on the teacher's voicemail. The message relates to a concern about a student and is directed at the teacher. The teacher should:

A. Call back immediately and confront the parent

B. Cool off, plan what to discuss with the parent, then call back

C. Question the child to find out what set off the parent

D. Ignore the message, since feelings of anger usually subside after a while

(Easy) (Skill 11.1)

103. Which of the following should *not* be a purpose of a parent–teacher conference?

A. To involve the parent in their child's education

B. To establish a friendship with the child's parents

C. To resolve a concern about the child's performance

D. To inform parents of positive behaviors by the child

(Easy) (Skill 11.1)

104. Mr. Brown wishes to improve his parent communication skills. Which of the following is a strategy he can utilize to accomplish this goal?

    A. Hold parent–teacher conferences

    B. Send home positive notes

    C. Have parent nights where the parents are invited into his classroom

    D. All of the above

(Average) (Skill 11.1)

105. Bobby, a nine-year-old, has been caught stealing frequently in the classroom. What might be a factor contributing to this behavior?

    A. Need for the items stolen

    B. Serious emotional disturbance

    C. Desire to experiment

    D. A normal stage of development

(Easy) (Skill 11.1)

106. Tommy is a student in your class; his parents are deaf. Tommy is struggling with math and you want to contact the parents to discuss the issues. How should you proceed?

    A. Limit contact due to the parents' inability to hear

    B. Use a TTY phone to communicate with the parents

    C. Talk to your administrator to find an appropriate interpreter to help you communicate with the parents personally

    D. Both B and C

(Average) (Skill 11.1)

107. According to recent studies, what is the estimated number of adolescents that have physical, social, or emotional problems related to the abuse of alcohol?

    A. Less than one million

    B. One to two million

    C. Two to three million

    D. Over four million

(Average) (Skill 11.1)

108. A child exhibits the following symptoms: a lack of emotional responsiveness, indifference to physical contact, abnormal social play, and abnormal speech. What is the likely diagnosis for this child?

    A. Separation anxiety

    B. Mental retardation

    C. Autism

    D. Hypochondria

(Rigorous) (Skill 11.2)

109. Mrs. Peck wants to justify the use of personalized learning communities to her principal. Which of the following reasons should she use?

    A. They build multiculturalism

    B. They provide a supportive environment to address academic and emotional needs

    C. They build relationships between students, which promotes lifelong learning

    D. They are proactive in their nature

(Easy) (Skill 11.2)

110. Johnny, a middle-schooler, comes to class uncharacteristically tired, distracted, withdrawn, and sullen and he cries easily. What should be the teacher's first response?

   A. Send him to the office to sit

   B. Call his parents

   C. Ask him what is wrong

   D. Ignore his behavior

(Average) (Skill 11.3)

111. What is an effective way to prepare students for testing?

   A. Minimize the importance of the test

   B. Orient the students to the test, telling them the purpose of the test, how the results will be used, and how it is relevant to them

   C. Use the same format for every test are given

   D. Have them construct an outline from which to study

(Rigorous) (Skill 11.7)

112. The data coordinator of the district who is concerned with federal funding for reading will probably want to start aggregating scores immediately because:

   A. The public has a right to know

   B. By aggregating, the individual scores can be combined to view performance trends across groups

   C. This will help the district determine which groups need more remedial instruction

   D. Both B and C

(Easy) (Skill 13.1)

113. When a teacher wants to utilize an assessment that is subjective in nature, which of the following is the most effective method for scoring?

   A. Rubric

   B. Checklist

   C. Alternative assessment

   D. Subjective measures should not be utilized

(Rigorous) (Skill 14.1)

114. Maria was an outstanding student in her elementary school in Brazil. Now she is nervous about starting fourth grade in the United States, although she learned English as a second language in Brazil. She and her parents should be relieved to know that:

   A. She will get extra help in the United States with her English

   B. There is a positive and strong correlation between a child's native language and his or her learning of English

   C. Her classmates will help her

   D. She will have a few months to study for the reading test

(Average) (Skill 14.1)

115. Safeguards against bias and discrimination in the assessment of children include:

   A. Testing the child in standard English

   B. Requiring the use of one standardized test

   C. Using evaluative materials in the child's native language or other mode of communication

   D. Requiring that tests be issued by a certified, licensed psychologist

(Easy) (Skill 14.1)

116. Which of the following is an accurate description of ESOL students?

    A. Remedial students

    B. Exceptional education students

    C. Not a homogeneous group

    D. Confident in communicating in English when with their peers

(Easy) (Skill 14.1)

117. What is one of the most important things to know about the differences between first language (L1) and second language (L2) acquisition?

    A. A second language is easier to acquire than a first language

    B. Most people master a second language (L2), but rarely do they master a first language (L1)

    C. Most people master a first language (L1), but rarely do they master a second language (L2)

    D. Acquiring a first language (L1) takes the same level of difficulty as acquiring a second language (L2)

(Rigorous) (Skill 14.1)

118. Etienne is an ESOL student. He has begun to engage in conversation that produces a connected narrative. What developmental stage for second language acquisition is he in?

    A. Early production

    B. Speech emergence

    C. Preproduction

    D. Intermediate fluency

(Average) (Skill 14.2)

119. Which of the following describes the functional approach to language acquisition?

    A. Focus on communicative elements

    B. Focus on conceptual purposes

    C. Focus on grammar elements

    D. All of the above

(Rigorous) (Skill 14.2)

120. Is it easier for ESOL students who read in their first language to learn to read in English?

    A. No, because the letter-sound relationships in English are unique

    B. Yes, because this will give the children confidence

    C. No, because there is often interference from one language to the next

    D. Yes, because the process is the same regardless of the language

Answer Key

1. B	15. C	29. C	43. D	57. B	71. C	85. D	99. C	113. A
2. B	16. A	30. C	44. B	58. D	72. B	86. B	100. B	114. B
3. B	17. B	31. D	45. D	59. D	73. B	87. A	101. D	115. C
4. D	18. B	32. B	46. C	60. B	74. B	88. D	102. B	116. C
5. D	19. B	33. C	47. B	61. A	75. C	89. B	103. B	117. C
6. D	20. C	34. D	48. C	62. A	76. D	90. C	104. D	118. D
7. D	21. C	35. C	49. A	63. D	77. B	91. A	105. B	119. A
8. B	22. C	36. C	50. B	64. C	78. D	92. A	106. D	120. D
9. B	23. B	37. D	51. B	65. A	79. C	93. D	107. D	
10. C	24. B	38. A	52. D	66. B	80. D	94. B	108. C	
11. A	25. B	39. D	53. A	67. D	81. D	95. A	109. B	
12. B	26. D	40. A	54. B	68. B	82. D	96. C	110. C	
13. A	27. C	41. B	55. D	69. B	83. D	97. C	111. B	
14. B	28. D	42. A	56. B	70. A	84. B	98. D	112. D	

Rigor Table

RIGOR TABLE	
Rigor level	**Questions**
Easy 20%	4, 11, 12, 16, 33, 34, 37, 42, 49, 58, 60, 66, 70, 72, 73, 74, 78, 80, 81, 82, 92, 96, 102, 103, 104, 106, 110, 113, 116, 117
Average 40%	1, 6, 7, 8, 14, 15, 17, 18, 19, 28, 30, 36, 38, 39, 44, 46, 48, 50, 51, 53, 54, 55, 57, 59, 61, 62, 65, 67, 69, 75, 76, 77, 79, 83, 85, 86, 89, 90, 94, 97, 98, 99, 101, 105, 107, 108, 111, 115, 119
Rigorous 40%	2, 3, 5, 9, 10, 13, 20, 21, 22, 23, 24, 25, 26, 27, 29, 31, 32, 35, 40, 41, 43, 45, 47, 52, 56, 63, 64, 68, 71, 84, 87, 88, 91, 93, 95, 100, 109, 112, 114, 118, 120

Sample Test with Rationales

(Average) (Skill 1.1)

1. **What would improve planning for instruction?**

   A. Describe the role of the teacher and student

   B. Evaluate the outcomes of instruction

   C. Rearrange the order of activities

   D. Give outside assignments

Answer: B. Evaluate the outcomes of instruction

As important as it is to plan content, materials, activities, and goals according to learner needs, the effort is in vain if students are not able to demonstrate improvement in the skills being taught. An important part of the planning process is for the teacher to continuously adapt all aspects of the curriculum to what is actually happening in the classroom. Planning frequently misses the mark or fails to allow for unexpected changes in circumstances. Regularly evaluating the outcomes of instruction and making adjustments accordingly will have a positive impact on the overall success of a teaching methodology.

(Rigorous) (Skill 1.1)

2. **What is the best definition for an achievement test?**

   A. It measures mechanical and practical abilities

   B. It measures broad areas of knowledge that are the result of cumulative learning experiences

   C. It measures the ability to learn to perform a task

   D. It measures performance related to specific, recently acquired information

Answer: B. It measures broad areas of knowledge that are the result of cumulative learning experiences

The ways that a teacher uses test data is a meaningful aspect of instruction and may increase motivation in students, especially when this information is available in the form of feedback to the students. This feedback should indicate to the students what they need to do in order to improve their achievement.

(Rigorous) (Skill 1.1)

3. **Norm-referenced tests:**

   A. Give information only about the local samples results

   B. Provide information about how the local test takers did compared to a representative sampling of national test takers

   C. Make no comparisons to national test takers

   D. None of the above

Answer: B. Provide information about how the local test takers did compared to a representative sampling of national test takers

This is the definition of a norm-referenced test.

(Easy) (Skill 1.1)

4. **A standardized test may be:**

    A. Given out with the same predetermined questions and format to all

    B. Given to certain children, but not all

    C. Taken over a lengthier test period if given out in exactly the same format with the same content

    D. All of the above

    Answer: D. All of the above

    All of the choices together make up the definition of a standardized test.

(Rigorous) (Skill 1.2)

5. **Which of the following describes why it is important and necessary for teachers to be able to analyze data on their students?**

    A. So that they can provide appropriate instruction

    B. So that they can make instructional decisions

    C. So that they can communicate and determine instructional progress

    D. All of the above

Answer: D. All of the above

Especially in today's high-stakes environment, it is critical that teachers have a complete understanding of the process involved in examining student data in order to make instructional decisions, prepare lessons, determine progress, and report progress to stakeholders.

(Average) (Skill 1.2)

6. **How are standardized tests useful in assessment?**

    A. For teacher evaluation

    B. For evaluation of the administration

    C. For comparison from school to school

    D. For comparison to the population on which the test was normed

Answer: D. For comparison to the population on which the test was normed.

While the efficacy of the standardized tests that are being used nationally has come under attack recently, they are currently the only devices for comparing where an individual student stands within a wide range of peers. They also provide a measure for a program or a school to evaluate how their own students are doing as compared to the populace at large. Even so, they should not be the only measure upon which decisions are made or evaluations drawn. There are many other instruments for measuring student achievement that the teacher needs to consult and take into account.

(Average) (Skill 1.3)

7. **What is evaluation of instructional activity based on?**

   A. Student grades

   B. Teacher evaluation

   C. Student participation

   D. Specified criteria

Answer: D. Specified criteria

The ways that a teacher uses test data is a meaningful aspect of instruction and may increase the motivation level of the students, especially when this information takes the form of feedback to the students. However, in order for a test to be an accurate measurement of student progress, the teacher must know how to plan and construct tests that reflect what is being taught throughout the year.

(Average) (Skill 1.3)

8. **What must be a consideration when a parent complains that he or she cannot control his or her child's behavior?**

   A. Whether the parent gives feedback to the child

   B. Whether the parent's expectations for control are developmentally appropriate

   C. How much time the parent spends with the child

   D. How rigid the rules are that the parent sets

Answer: B. Whether the parent's expectations for control are developmentally appropriate

The teacher is the expert when it comes to developmental expectations. This is one area where a concerned and helpful teacher can be invaluable in helping a family through a crisis. Parents often have unrealistic expectations about their children's behavior simply because they don't know what is average for a particular age group and what is not. A teacher can help to diffuse conflicts in these cases.

(Rigorous) (Skill 1.3)

9. **If teachers attend to content, instructional materials, activities, learner needs, and goals in instructional planning, what could be an outcome?**

   A. Planning for the next year

   B. Effective classroom performance

   C. Elevated test scores on standardized tests

   D. More student involvement

Answer: B. Effective classroom performance

Efficient instructional planning leads to easy-to-manage classrooms and higher student achievement.

(Rigorous) (Skill 1.4)

10. **Mrs. Grant provides her students with many extrinsic motivators in order to increase their intrinsic motivation. Which of the following best explains this relationship?**

    A. This is a good relationship, and it will increase intrinsic motivation

    B. This relationship builds animosity between the teacher and the students

    C. Extrinsic motivation alone does not help to build intrinsic motivation

    D. There is no place for extrinsic motivation in the classroom

    Answer: C. Extrinsic motivation alone does not help to build intrinsic motivation

    There are some cases where it is necessary to utilize extrinsic motivation; however, the use of extrinsic motivation alone is not an effective strategy to build intrinsic motivation. Intrinsic motivation comes from within the student themselves.

(Easy) (Skill 1.4)

11. **Which of the following is considered a study skill?**

    A. Using graphs, tables, and maps

    B. Using a desktop publishing program

    C. Explaining important vocabulary words

    D. Asking for clarification

    Answer: A. Using graphs, tables, and maps

    In studying, it is certainly true that "a picture is worth a thousand words." Not only are these devices useful in making a point clear, they are excellent mnemonic devices for remembering facts.

(Easy) (Skill 1.4)

12. **Which of the following test items is not objective?**

    A. Multiple choice

    B. Essay

    C. Matching

    D. True/false

    Answer: B. Essay

    Although essays can be used to demonstrate a student's critical thinking skills, it is not considered an objective test because there is no single correct answer (unlike multiple choice, matching, and true/false).

(Rigorous) (Skill 2.1)

13. **What should a teacher do when students do not respond well to an instructional activity?**

    A. Reevaluate learner needs

    B. Request administrative help

    C. Continue with the activity another day

    D. Assign homework on the concept

Answer: A. Reevaluate learner needs

After a lesson is carefully planned, teacher observation is the single most important component of an instructional presentation. These observations will drive the lesson and determine the direction that the lesson will take, based on student activity and behavior. For example, if the teacher observes that a particular student is not on-task, she may change from a teacher-directed approach to a more interactive approach.

(Average) (Skill 2.1)

14. **Why is it important for a teacher to pose a question before calling on students to answer?**

    A. It helps manage student conduct

    B. It keeps the students as a group focused on the class work

    C. It allows students time to collaborate

    D. It gives the teacher time to walk among the students

    Answer: B. It keeps the students as a group focused on the class work

    It doesn't take much distraction for a class's attention to become diffused, so the teacher should plan presentations that will keep students focused on the lesson. A very useful tool is effective, well-thought-out, pointed questions.

(Average) (Skill 2.1)

15. **Which statement is an example of specific praise?**

    A. "John, you are the only person in class not paying attention."

    B. "William, I thought we agreed that you would turn in all of your homework."

    C. "Robert, you did a good job staying in line. See how it helped us get to music class on time?"

    D. "Class, you did a great job cleaning up the art room."

    Answer: C. "Robert, you did a good job staying in line. See how it helped us get to music class on time?"

    Praise is a powerful tool in obtaining and maintaining order in a classroom. It is also an effective motivator. It is even more effective if the positive results of good behavior are included.

(Easy) (Skill 2.1)

16. **What is one way a teacher can supplement verbal praise?**

    A. Help students evaluate their own performance and supply self-reinforcement

    B. Give verbal praise more frequently

    C. Give tangible rewards such as stickers or treats

    D. Have students practice giving verbal praise

Answer: A. Help students evaluate their own performance and supply self-reinforcement

While praise is useful in maintaining order in a classroom and motivating students, it's important for the teacher to remember at all times that students must be prepared to succeed in the world once the supports of the classroom are gone. Self-esteem, or lack thereof, is often a barrier to success. An important skill for students to learn is how to bolster one's own self-esteem and confidence.

(Average) (Skill 2.1)

17. **The teacher states that students will review the material from the previous day, demonstrate an electronic circuit, and set up an electronic circuit in small groups. What has the teacher demonstrated?**

   A. The importance of reviewing

   B. Giving the general framework for the lesson to facilitate learning

   C. Giving students the opportunity to leave if they are not interested in the lesson

   D. Providing momentum for the lesson

Answer: B. Giving the general framework for the lesson to facilitate learning

If children know where the lesson is going, they're more likely to be engaged in getting there. It's important to give them a road map whenever possible for what is coming in their classes.

(Average) (Skill 2.1)

18. **What is one benefit of amplifying a student's response?**

   A. It helps the student develop a positive self-image

   B. It is helpful to other students who are in the process of learning the reasoning or steps in answering the question

   C. It allows the teacher to cover more content

   D. It helps to keep the information organized

Answer: B. It is helpful to other students who are in the process of learning the reasoning or steps in answering the question

Not only does the teacher show acceptance and give value to student responses by acknowledging, amplifying, discussing, or restating the comment or question, she also helps the rest of the class learn to reason. If a student response is allowed, even if it is blurted out, it must be acknowledged and the student made aware of the quality of the response.

(Average) (Skill 2.1)

19. **How can the teacher help students become more work-oriented and less disruptive?**

   A. Seek their input for content instruction

   B. Challenge the students with a task and show genuine enthusiasm for it

   C. Use behavior modification techniques with all students

   D. Make sure lesson plans are complete for the week

Answer: B. Challenge the students with a task and show genuine enthusiasm for it

Many studies have demonstrated a teacher's enthusiasm is infectious. If students feel that the teacher is ambivalent about a task they will also catch that attitude.

(Rigorous) (Skill 2.1)

20. **What is an established method for increasing student originality, intrinsic motivation, and higher-order thinking skills?**

    A. Painting the walls a neutral color

    B. Setting high expectations

    C. Providing student choice

    D. Use of authentic learning opportunities

Answer: C. Student choice

It has been shown through research that providing student choice can increase all of the described factors because it gives students the chance to demonstrate what they have learned.

(Rigorous) (Skill 2.1)

21. **Why is it important for the teacher to alert nonperformers when conducting activities?**

    A. It creates suspense

    B. Students will take over the discipline

    C. Students will become more work involved

    D. Students will more likely not take part in the recitation

Answer: C. Students will become more work involved

Students are eager to shift into neutral gear when they are not specifically involved in an activity, which is a waste of classroom time for those students. The teacher needs to find ways to keep them involved in what is going on, even if they are only spectators. A good way to do this is to alert them that they may be called on for an answer and therefore must pay attention.

(Rigorous) (Skill 2.1)

22. **Ms. Smith says, "Exactly what do you mean by, 'It was the author's intention to mislead you'?" What does this illustrate?**

    A. Digression

    B. Restating a response

    C. Probing a response

    D. Amplifying a response

Answer: C. Probing a response

Educational researchers and practitioners generally agree that teachers' effective use of questioning promotes student learning because it encourages student participation and gives value to student responses.

(Rigorous) (Skill 2.1)

23. **What is a frequently used type of feedback to students?**

    A. Correctives

    B. Confirmation

    C. Correcting the response

    D. Explanations

Answer: B. Confirmation

Even if the student's answer is not perfect, there are always ways to praise him and make use of his answer unless, of course, he was deliberately answering wrongly. When a behavior is praised, it is likely to be repeated.

(Rigorous) (Skill 2.1)

24. **What is the definition of a nonperformer?**

    A. Students who are off-task

    B. Students not chosen to answer a teacher-posed question

    C. Students with stanine scores of 20 or below

    D. Students who consistently score below 50 percent on classroom tests

Answer: B. Students not chosen to answer a teacher-posed question

Not all students can answer every question; however, the teacher should ensure that all students participate and that no student is permitted to be passive in all discussion periods.

(Rigorous) (Skill 2.1)

25. **What is *not* a way that teachers show acceptance and give value to a student response?**

    A. Acknowledging

    B. Correcting

    C. Discussing

    D. Amplifying

Answer: B. Correcting

There are ways to treat every answer as worthwhile, even if it happens to be wrong. The objective is to keep students involved in the dialogue. If their efforts to participate are "rewarded" with what seems to them to be a rebuke or a comment that leads to embarrassment, they will be less willing to respond the next time.

(Rigorous) (Skill 2.1)

26. **What is teacher with-it-ness?**

    A. Having adequate knowledge of subject matter

    B. A skill that must be mastered to attain certification

    C. Understanding the current fads and trends that affect students

    D. When a teacher gives a sense that she knows what she is doing

Answer: D. When a teacher gives a sense that she knows what she is doing

The teacher who knows his or her class well and is "with-it" will be cognizant of what is happening in every corner of the classroom between and among the children at all times. The "with-it" teacher frequently knows when and why problems will occur and will act to eliminate potential provocation.

(Rigorous) (Skill 2.1)

27. The teacher responds, "Yes, that is correct" to a student's answer. What is this an example of?

    A. Academic feedback

    B. Academic praise

    C. Simple positive response

    D. Simple negative response

Answer: C. Simple positive response

Academic feedback and simple negative responses are not methods of giving praise. Academic praise is a group of specific statements that give information about the value of the response or its implications. For example, a teacher using academic praise would respond, "That is an excellent analysis of Twain's use of the river in *Huckleberry Finn*," whereas a simple positive response to the same question would be, "That's correct."

(Average) (Skill 2.1)

28. **What are teacher redirects?**

    A. When the teacher redirects deviant behavior to another task

    B. When the teacher changes the focus of the class to provide smooth transitions

    C. When the teacher changes student jobs every nine weeks

    D. When the teacher asks a second student to expound on the first student's answer

Answer: D. The teacher asks a second student to expound on the first student's answer

When a student response is incorrect, it is difficult to maintain academic focus. The teacher must maintain focus on the task at hand and, at the same time, not devalue the student response. A good way of doing this is to ask another student to respond to the student who provided the incorrect answer, called *redirecting*.

(Rigorous) (Skill 2.2)

29. **When is the optimal benefit reached when handling an incorrect student response?**

    A. When graded work is returned to the student

    B. When the other students are allowed to correct that student

    C. When the student understands how to use the feedback

    D. When the teacher asks simple questions, provides cues to clarify, or gives assistance for working out the correct response

Answer: C. When the student understands how to use the feedback

When students receive feedback on their work, either verbally or in writing, it strengthens learning. It's important that students feel confident and comfortable in making responses, knowing that even if they give a wrong answer, they will not be embarrassed. One way to respond to the incorrect answer is to ask the student, "Show me from your book why you think that." This gives the student a chance to correct the answer and redeem himself or herself. Learning opportunities are lost when teachers only provide a numerical grade for assignments. Teachers can ask students to do additional things to work with their original products, like take small sections and rewrite based on the feedback, or use a rubric to self-score the assignment. While written feedback will enhance student learning, having students do something with the feedback encourages an even deeper learning and reflection.

(Average) (Skill 2.3)

30. **The effective teacher communicates nonverbally with students by:**

    A. Writing directions on the board

    B. Using facial expressions to express dissatisfaction instead of correcting the student verbally

    C. Using positive body language and expressing warmth, concern, and acceptance

    D. Not making eye contact with students

    Answer: C. Using positive body language and expressing warmth, concern, and acceptance

    Effective teachers augment their instructional presentations by using positive nonverbal communication such as smiles, open body posture, movement, and eye contact with students. The energy and enthusiasm of the effective teacher can be amplified through positive body language.

(Rigorous) (Skill 2.3)

31. **Efficient use of time includes which of the following?**

    A. Daily review, seatwork, and recitation of concepts

    B. Lesson initiation, transition, and comprehension check

    C. Review, test, review

    D. Punctuality and management transition

    Answer: D. Punctuality and management transition

    While the other activities listed can be effective teaching methods, punctuality and management transition are key in using time efficiently. Punctuality allows the teacher to cover all planned material in the allotted time; management transition prevents students from being distracted and slowed down by transitions in activities.

(Rigorous) (Skill 2.3)

32. **In a success-oriented classroom, mistakes are viewed as:**

    A. Motivations to improve

    B. A natural part of the learning process

    C. Ways to improve

    D. Building blocks

    Answer: B. A natural part of the learning process

    In the success-oriented classroom, mistakes are viewed as a natural part of learning. With this approach, students have the opportunity to learn by correcting mistakes, rather than seeing the mistake as a penalty.

(Easy) (Skill 2.3)

33. **Which of the following can affect the desire of students to learn new material?**

    A. Assessment plans

    B. Lesson plans

    C. Enthusiasm

    D. School community

Answer: C. Enthusiasm

The enthusiasm a teacher exhibits not only has a positive effect on students' desire to learn, it encourages on-task behaviors as well.

(Easy) (Skill 2.3)

34. **A teacher's posture and movement affect the following student outcomes *except*:**

    A. Student learning

    B. Attitudes

    C. Motivation

    D. Physical development

Answer: D. Physical development

Studies show that a teacher's posture and movement are indicators of his or her enthusiasm and energy, which emphatically influence student outcomes including learning, attitudes, motivation, and focus on goals.

(Rigorous) (Skill 2.3)

35. **What is proactive classroom management?**

    A. Management that is constantly changing

    B. Management that is downplayed

    C. Management that gives clear and explicit instructions and rewarding compliance

    D. Management that is designed by the students

Answer: C. Management that gives clear and explicit instructions and rewards compliance

Classroom management plans should be in place when the school year begins. Developing a management plan takes a proactive approach—that is, deciding what behaviors will be expected of the class as a whole, anticipating possible problems, and teaching appropriate behaviors early in the school year. Acknowledging compliance increases the likelihood that the positive behavior will continue.

(Average) (Skill 2.4)

36. **What is the most significant development emerging in children at age two?**

    A. Immune system develops

    B. Socialization occurs

    C. Language develops

    D. Perception develops

Answer: C. Language develops

Language begins to develop in an infant not long after birth. Chomsky claims that children teach themselves to speak using the people around them for resources. Several studies of the sounds infants make in their cribs seem to support this.

(Easy) (Skill 2.4)

37. **When communicating with parents for whom English is not the primary language, you should:**

    A. Provide materials whenever possible in their native language

    B. Use an interpreter

    C. Provide the same communication as you would to native English-speaking parents

    D. All of the above

Answer: D. All of the above

When communicating with non-English-speaking parents it is important to treat them as you would any other parent and utilize any means necessary to ensure they have the ability to participate in their child's educational process.

(Average) (Skill 2.4)

38. **What has research shown to be the effect of using advance organizers in the lesson?**

    A. They facilitate learning and retention

    B. They enhance retention only

    C. They only serve to help the teacher organize the lesson

    D. They show definitive positive results on student achievement

Answer: A. They facilitate learning and retention

J.M. Kallison, Jr., found subject matter retention increased when lessons included an outline at the beginning of the lesson and a summary at the end of the lesson. This type of structure is utilized in successful classrooms.

(Average) (Skill 3.1)

39. **In promoting professional development opportunities for teachers that enhance student achievement, the following must be considered:**

    A. Teachers must be provided time to complete the training at minimal cost

    B. Teachers must use data to choose training that correlates with areas of student needs

    C. Teachers must complete required training hours to maintain their teacher certification

    D. All of the above

Answer: D. All of the above

Teachers in Florida are required to earn a minimum of 6 college credits or 120 in-service points every five years to renew their teaching certification. In order to promote the vision, mission, and action plans of school communities, teachers must be given the toolkits to maximize instructional performance. It is vital to provide teachers with the time to analyze student data and then to provide training courses to prepare teachers to meet those students needs.

(Rigorous) (Skill 3.1)

40. In reviewing FCAT reading scores for his current students, Mr. Garcia finds that 40 percent of his students failed to meet standards on main idea and purpose. Which of the following professional development activities should Mr. Garcia choose to improve achievement for his current students?

    A. Comprehension reading strategies

    B. Vocabulary development

    C. Behavior management

    D. FCAT test preparation

    Answer: A. Comprehension reading strategies

    To enhance student achievement, teachers must use student data to reflect on current teaching practices and determine training that will strengthen instruction in the areas of need. Because Mr. Garcia's students struggle with main idea, he should choose training in the area of reading comprehension strategies.

(Rigorous) (Skill 3.2)

41. Mr. Graham has taken the time to reflect, complete observations, and ask for feedback about the interactions between him and his students from his principal. It is obvious by seeking this information out that Mr. Graham understands which of the following?

    A. The importance of clear communication with the principal

    B. That he needs to analyze the effectiveness of his classroom interactions

    C. That he is clearly communicating with the principal

    D. That he cares about his students

    Answer: B. That he needs to analyze the effectiveness of his classroom interactions

    Utilizing reflection, observations, and feedback from peers or supervisors, teachers can help to build their own understanding of how they interact with students. In this way, they can better analyze their effectiveness at building appropriate relationships with students.

(Easy) (Skill 3.2)

42. Which of the following is a good reason to collaborate with a peer?

    A. To increase your knowledge in areas where you feel you are weak, but the peer is strong

    B. To increase your planning time and that of your peer by combining the classes and taking more breaks

    C. To have fewer lesson plans to write

    D. To teach fewer subjects

    Answer: A. To increase your knowledge in areas where you feel you are weak, but the peer is strong

    Collaboration with a peer allows teachers to share ideas and information. In this way, the teachers are able to improve their skills and share additional information with each other.

(Rigorous) (Skill 3.2)

43. **Which of the following are ways a professional can assess his or her teaching strengths and weaknesses?**

    A. Examining how many students are unable to understand a concept

    B. Asking peers for suggestions or ideas

    C. Self-evaluation/reflection of lessons taught

    D. All of the above

Answer: D. All of the above

It is important for teachers to involve themselves in constant periods of reflection and self-reflection to ensure that they are meeting the needs of the students.

(Average) (Skill 4.1)

44. **Which of the following might improve planning for instruction?**

    A. Describing the role of the teacher and student

    B. Evaluating the outcomes of instruction

    C. Rearranging the order of activities

    D. Giving outside assignments

Answer: B. Evaluating the outcomes of instruction

An important part of the planning process is for the teacher to constantly adapt all aspects of the curriculum to what is actually happening in the classroom. Planning frequently misses the mark or fails to allow for unexpected events. Evaluating the outcomes of instruction regularly and making adjustments accordingly will have a positive impact on the overall success of a teaching methodology.

(Rigorous) (Skill 4.1)

45. **The professional teacher provides realistic projects and problem solving activities that will enable all students to demonstrate their ability to think creatively. Which of the following is an example of a project that will develop critical thinking?**

    A. Ask students to list items they would purchase from a catalog

    B. Ask students to determine total cost of order from the catalog

    C. Ask students to find another source for purchasing the items

    D. Ask students to compare shopping ads or catalog deals

Answer: D. Ask students to compare shopping ads or catalog deals

While all of these activities allow students to experience learning in a realistic, real-world setting (shopping for items), only answer choice D moves students to higher levels of thinking. Asking students to list items is at the Knowledge level on Bloom's taxonomy. Students will move to the Comprehension level of Bloom's when they must determine total cost or find another source for the items. But when asked to compare the ads, student are moved to the Synthesis level of Bloom's.

(Average) (Skill 4.1)

46. **Which of the following is *not* one of the levels of Bloom's taxonomy?**

    A. Synthesis

    B. Evaluation

    C. Understanding

    D. Knowledge

Answer: C. Understanding

Bloom's taxonomy consists of the following levels: Knowledge, Comprehension, Application, Analysis, Synthesis, and Evaluation. These levels are in order from the most basic level to the more complex.

(Rigorous) (Skill 4.1)

47. **Mr. Ryan has proposed to his classroom that the students may demonstrate understanding of the unit taught in a variety of ways, including taking a test, writing a paper, creating an oral presentation, or building a model/project. Which of the following areas of differentiation has Mr. Ryan demonstrated?**

    A. Synthesis

    B. Product

    C. Content

    D. Process

Answer: B. Product

There are three ways to differentiate instruction: content, process, and product. In the described case, Mr. Ryan has chosen to provide the students with alternate opportunities to produce knowledge; therefore, the product is the area being differentiated.

(Average) (Skill 4.1)

48. **What is an example of a low-order question?**

    A. Why is it important to recycle items in your home?

    B. Compare how glass and plastics are recycled.

    C. What items do we recycle in our county?

    D. Explain the importance of recycling in our county.

Answer: C. What items do we recycle in our county?

Low-order questions refer to specific answers about concrete items, while higher-order questions refer to concepts that are more in the abstract.

(Easy) (Skill 4.1)

49. **What is the most important benefit of students developing critical thinking skills?**

    A. Students are able to apply knowledge to a specific subject area as well as other subject areas

    B. Students remember the information for testing purposes

    C. Students focus on a limited number of specific facts

    D. Students do not have to memorize the information for later recall

Answer: A. Students are able to apply knowledge to a specific subject area as well as other subject areas

When a student learns to think critically, he or she learns how to apply knowledge to a specific subject area; but more important, the student knows how to apply that information in other subject areas.

(Average) (Skill 4.1)

50. **When is content teaching effective?**

    A. When it is presented in demonstration form

    B. When the teacher separates the content into distinct elements

    C. When the content is covered over a long span of time

    D. When the decision about content is made at the district level

Answer: B. When the teacher separates the content into distinct elements

Students of all ages can absorb material that is focused better than material that is diffuse. Structuring the presentation of new material by topic and staying on target within each component is the most effective way to communicate material.

(Average) (Skill 4.2)

51. **Wait-time has what effect?**

    A. Gives structure to the class discourse

    B. Fewer chain and low-level questions are asked with more higher-level questions included

    C. Gives the students time to evaluate the response

    D. Gives the opportunity for in-depth discussion about the topic

Answer: B. Fewer chain and low-level questions are asked with more higher-level questions included

One part of the questioning process for the successful teacher is *wait-time*: the time between the question and either the student response or your follow-up. Many teachers vaguely recommend some general amount of wait-time (until the student starts to get uncomfortable or is clearly perplexed), but we focus here on wait-time as a specific and powerful communicative tool that speaks through its structured silences. Embedded in wait-time are subtle clues about your judgments of a student's abilities and your expectations of individuals and groups. For example, the more time you allow a student to mull through a question, the more you trust his or her ability to answer that question without getting flustered. As a rule, the practice of prompting is not a problem. Giving support and helping students reason through difficult conundrums is part of being an effective teacher.

(Rigorous) (Skill 4.2)

52. **Teachers who want to improve creative thinking in their students can use which of the following strategies?**

    A. Increase wait time to 5 seconds

    B. Ask deliberate questions

    C. Ask students to journal and reflect on what they just learned

    D. All of the above

Answer: D. All of the above

Planning and asking deliberate questions that are not simple recall questions and increasing wait time after asking a question allows students time to process the question and formulate a more complex answer. Giving students time to write and reflect on new learning allows the same opportunity.

(Average) (Skill 5.1)

53. **How can the teacher establish a positive climate in the classroom?**

    A. Help students see the positive aspects of various cultures

    B. Use whole group instruction for all content areas

    C. Help students divide into cooperative groups based on ability

    D. Eliminate teaching strategies that allow students to make choices

    Answer: A. Help students see the positive aspects of various cultures

    An important purpose of education is to prepare students to live successfully in the real world and appreciating different cultures will prepare them for a wide range of contexts and interactions. Additionally, the most fertile learning environment is one in which all viewpoints and backgrounds are respected.

(Average) (Skill 5.1)

54. **What do cooperative learning methods all have in common?**

    A. Multiple intelligence philosophy

    B. Cooperative task/cooperative reward structures

    C. Student roles and communication

    D. Teacher-centered roles

    Answer: B. Cooperative task/cooperative reward structures

    Cooperative learning situations, as practiced in today's classrooms, grew out of searches conducted by several groups in the early 1970s. Cooperative learning situations can range from very formal applications, such as STAD (Student Teams-Achievement Divisions) and CIRC (Cooperative Integrated Reading and Composition), to less formal groupings known variously as "group investigation," "learning together," and "discovery groups." Cooperative learning as a general term is now firmly recognized and established as a teaching and learning technique in American schools. Because cooperative learning techniques are so widely diffused in the schools, it is necessary to orient students in the skills by which cooperative learning groups can operate smoothly and, thereby, enhance learning. Students who cannot interact constructively with other students will not be able to take advantage of the learning opportunities provided by the cooperative learning situations and will furthermore deprive their fellow students of the opportunity for cooperative learning.

(Average) (Skill 5.2)

55. **What is a good strategy for teaching a group of ethnically diverse students?**

    A. Don't focus on the students' culture

    B. Expect them to assimilate easily into your classroom

    C. Imitate their speech patterns

    D. Include ethnic studies in the curriculum

Answer: D. Include ethnic studies in the curriculum

Exploring students' own cultures increases their confidence levels in the group. It is also a very useful tool when students are struggling to develop identities that they can feel comfortable with. An added benefit is that this prepares students for life outside the classroom.

(Rigorous) (Skill 6.1)

56. **What developmental patterns should a professional teacher assess to meet the needs of the student?**

   A. Academic, regional, and family background

   B. Social, physical, and academic

   C. Academic, physical, and family background

   D. Physical, family, and ethnic background

Answer: B. Social, physical, and academic

The effective teacher applies knowledge of physical, social, and academic developmental patterns and of individual differences to meet the instructional needs of all students in the classroom. The most important premise of child development is that all domains of development (social, physical, and academic) are integrated. An examination of the student's file coupled with ongoing evaluation ensures a successful educational experience for both teacher and students.

(Average) (Skill 6.2)

57. **According to the Principles of Professional Conduct for the Education Profession in Florida, an individual educator's certificate can be revoked or suspended if the following happens:**

   A. Teacher is accused of hurting a child

   B. Teacher fails to self-report within forty-eight (48) hours to appropriate authorities (as determined by district) any arrests/charges involving the abuse of a child

   C. Teacher uses curse words in front of a parent

   D. Teacher fails to attend mandatory training

Answer: B. Teacher fails to self-report within forty-eight (48) hours to appropriate authorities (as determined by district) any arrests/charges involving the abuse of a child

All reports of injury to a child should be investigated thoroughly. At times, teachers are falsely accused. However, the law is very clear that any teacher who is arrested or charged with child abuse must self report this arrest within 48 hours. Such notice shall not be considered an admission of guilt nor shall such notice be admissible for any purpose in any proceeding, civil or criminal, administrative or judicial, investigatory or adjudicatory.

(Easy) (Skill 6.2)

58. **Teachers must hold themselves to high standards. When they engage in negative actions such as fighting with students, they are violating all of the following except:**

    A. Ethics

    B. Professionalism

    C. Morals

    D. Fiscal

Answer: D. Fiscal

Teachers must adhere to strict rules and regulations to maintain the highest degree of conduct and professionalism in the classroom. Current court cases in Florida have examined ethical violations of teachers engaged in improper communication and abuse with students, along with teachers engaged in drug violations and substance abuse in classrooms. It is imperative that today's teachers have the highest regard for professionalism and behave as proper role models for students in and out of the classroom.

(Average) (Skill 7.1)

59. **Students who can solve problems mentally have:**

    A. Reached maturity

    B. Physically developed

    C. Reached the preoperational stage of thought

    D. Achieved the ability to manipulate objects symbolically

Answer: D. Achieved the ability to manipulate objects symbolically

When students are able to solve mental problems, it is an indication to the teacher that they have achieved the ability to manipulate objects symbolically, and they should be instructed to continue to develop their cognitive and academic skills.

(Easy) (Skill 7.1)

60. **Mrs. Potts is in the middle of her math lesson, but notices that many of her students seem to be having some sort of difficulty. Mrs. Potts stops class and decides to have a class meeting. Although her math objectives are important, it is equally important to address whatever is troubling her classroom. This is because:**

    A. Discipline is important

    B. Social issues can impact academic learning

    C. Maintaining order is important

    D. Social skills instruction is important

Answer: B. Social issues can impact academic learning

Mrs. Potts understands that as long as there is a social situation or issue in the classroom, it is unlikely that any academics she presents will be learned. All of those areas instructed are important; however, it is this understanding of the fact that the academics will be impacted that is important in this particular situation as she is interrupting her math instruction.

(Average) (Skill 7.1)

61. **When seeking the successful inclusion of students with disabilities:**

    A. A variety of instructional arrangements are available

    B. School personnel shift the responsibility for learning outcomes to the student

    C. The physical facilities are used as they are

    D. Regular classroom teachers have sole responsibility for evaluating student progress

    Answer: A. A variety of instructional arrangements are available

    All schools have policies and resources in place to aid in the inclusion of students with disabilities. Successful inclusion is possible when teachers employ these resources and maintain a positive attitude.

(Average) (Skill 7.2)

62. **Which of the following is not a communication issue that is related to diversity within the classroom?**

    A. Learning disorder

    B. Sensitive terminology

    C. Body language

    D. Discussing differing viewpoints and opinions

    Answer: A. Learning disorders

    While a learning disorder may affect the communication skills of a specific student, learning disorders are not in and of themselves a communication issue related to diversity within the classroom.

(Rigorous) (Skill 7.3)

63. **When are students more likely to understand complex ideas?**

    A. If they do outside research before coming to class

    B. When they write out the definitions of complex words

    C. When they attend a lecture on the subject

    D. When the ideas are clearly defined by the teacher and students are given examples and nonexamples of the concept

    Answer: D. When the ideas are clearly defined by the teacher and students are given examples and nonexamples of the concept

    Several studies have conclusively found that the most effective method of concept presentation included giving a definition along with examples and nonexamples and also providing an explanation of them.

(Rigorous) (Skill 7.3)

64. **What have recent studies regarding effective teachers concluded?**

    A. Effective teachers let students establish rules

    B. Effective teachers establish routines by the sixth week of school

    C. Effective teachers state their own policies and establish consistent class rules and procedures on the first day of class

    D. Effective teachers establish flexible routines

Answer: C. Effective teachers state their own policies and establish consistent class rules and procedures on the first day of class

The teacher can get ahead of the game by stating clearly on the first day of school exactly what the rules are. Establishing limits early and consistently enforcing them prevents distractions and enhances learning. The combination of conspicuously displayed rules, frequent verbal references to the rules, and appropriate consequences for appropriate behaviors leads to increased levels of on-task behavior.

(Average) (Skill 7.3)

65. **When is utilization of instructional materials most effective?**

   A. When the activities are sequenced

   B. When the materials are prepared ahead of time

   C. When the students choose the pages to work on

   D. When the students create the instructional materials

Answer: A. When the activities are sequenced

Most assignments will require more than one educational principle. It is helpful to explain to students the proper order in which these principles must be applied; disrupting the sequence can confuse students and prevent them from absorbing the material.

(Easy) (Skill 7.3)

66. **If teachers attend to content, instructional materials, activities, learner needs, and goals in instructional planning, what could be an outcome?**

   A. Planning for the next year

   B. Effective classroom performance

   C. Elevated test scores on standardized tests

   D. More student involvement

Answer: B. Effective classroom performance

Another outcome will be teacher satisfaction in a job well-done and in the performance of her students. Her days will have far fewer disruptions and her classroom will be easy to manage.

(Average) (Skill 7.3)

67. **When creating and selecting materials for instruction, teachers should complete which of the following steps:**

   A. Ensure material is relevant to the prior knowledge of the students

   B. Allow for a variation of learning styles

   C. Choose alternative teaching strategies

   D. All of the above

Answer: D. All of the above

It is imperative when creating and selecting materials for instruction that teachers consider many different factors. This makes the planning for instruction a difficult and somewhat time-consuming process. However, the steps listed above are crucial in teaching effectively.

(Rigorous) (Skill 7.3)

68. The teacher states, "We will work on the first page of vocabulary words. On the second page we will work on the structure and meaning of the words. We will go over these together and then you will write out the answers to the exercises on your own. I will be circulating to give help if needed." What is this an example of?

A. Evaluation of instructional activity

B. Analysis of instructional activity

C. Identification of expected outcomes

D. Pacing of instructional activity

Answer: B. Analysis of instructional activity

The successful teacher carefully plans all activities to foresee any difficulties in executing the plan. This assures that the directions being given to students will be clear and avoid any misunderstanding.

(Average) (Skill 7.4)

69. Which of the following is not a stage in Piaget's theory of child development?

A. Sensory motor stage

B. Preoptimal stage

C. Concrete operational

D. Formal operational

Answer: B. Preoptimal stage

Jean Piaget believed students passed through a series of stages to develop from the most basic forms of concrete thinking to sophisticated levels of abstract thinking. His developmental theory consists of four learning stages, which can be remembered with the following pneumonic: Stages Precious Children Follow (SPCF)

1. Sensory motor stage (from birth to age 2)

2. Preoperation stage (ages 2 to 7 or early elementary)

3. Concrete operational (ages 7 to 11 or upper elementary)

4. Formal operational (ages 7 to 15 or late elementary/high school)

(Easy) (Skill 7.4)

70. Constructivist classrooms are considered to be:

A. Student-centered

B. Teacher-centered

C. Focused on standardized tests

D. Requiring little creativity

Answer: A. Student-centered

Student-centered classrooms are considered to be "constructivist," in that students are given opportunities to construct their own meanings onto new pieces of knowledge.

(Rigorous) (Skill 7.4)

71. **Mr. Rogers describes his educational philosophy as eclectic, meaning that he uses many educational theories to guide his classroom practice. Why is this the best approach for today's teachers?**

    A. Today's classrooms are often too diverse for one theory to meet the needs of all students

    B. Educators must be able to draw upon other strategies if one theory is not effective

    C. Both A and B

    D. None of the above

    Answer: C. Both A and B

    No one theory will work for every classroom; a good approach is for an educator to incorporate a range of learning theories in his or her practice. Still, under the guidance of any good theory, good educators will differentiate their instructional practices to meet the needs of individual students' abilities and interests using various instructional practices.

(Easy) (Skill 7.4)

72. **How many stages of intellectual development does Piaget define?**

    A. Two

    B. Four

    C. Six

    D. Eight

    Answer: B. Four

    The stages are the sensorimotor stage, the preoperational stage, the concrete operational stage, and the formal operational stage.

(Easy) (Skill 7.4)

73. **Who developed the theory of multiple intelligences?**

    A. Bruner

    B. Gardner

    C. Kagan

    D. Cooper

    Answer: B. Gardner

    The Multiple Intelligence Theory, developed by Howard Gardner, suggests that students learn in at least seven different ways: visually/spatially, musically, verbally, logically/mathematically, interpersonally, intrapersonally, and bodily/kinesthetically.

(Easy) (Skill 7.5)

74. **Which of the following is a presentation modification?**

    A. Taking an assessment in an alternate room

    B. Providing an interpreter to give the test in American Sign Language

    C. Allowing dictation of written responses

    D. Extending the time limits on an assessment

    Answer: B. Providing an interpreter to give the test in American Sign Language

    There are numerous types of modifications that can be provided to students in the classroom and for assessments. All of the answer choices describe appropriate modifications, but the only one that affects the presentation of the items is the one related to providing an interpreter.

(Average) (Skill 7.5)

75. Free appropriate education, the individual education program, procedural safeguards, and least restrictive environment; identify the legislation represented by these elements.

    A. American with Disabilities Act

    B. The Equal Access Act

    C. The Individuals with Disabilities Education Act

    D. Title VI, The Civil Rights Act of 1964

Answer: C. The Individuals with Disabilities Education Act

The Individuals with Disabilities Education Act (IDEA) requires that all states receiving federal funding provide mandatory education programs for students with disabilities. P.L. 94-142 was reenacted as IDEA and the elements listed represent its key concepts.

(Average) (Skill 8.1)

76. Mr. Sanchez is having his students work with one-syllable words, removing the first consonant and substituting another, as in changing mats to hats. What reading skill are they working on?

    A. Morphemic inflections

    B. Pronouncing short vowels

    C. Invented spelling

    D. Phonemic awareness

Answer: D. Phonemic awareness

Phonemic awareness is the acknowledgement of sounds and words; a child's realization that some words rhyme is one of the skills that fall under this category.

(Average) (Skill 8.1)

77. Ms. James is seated with a child by her side. The child is reading aloud from an open book. Ms. James is teaching in a school that has embraced the balanced literacy approach. Therefore it is most likely that Ms. James is recording:

    A. The child's use of expression in reading aloud

    B. The child's errors and miscues

    C. Her observations of the child's attitude toward reading

    D. The child's feelings about the particular passage being read

Answer: B. The child's errors and miscues

The balanced literacy approach uses several different methods to help children develop their reading skills, including guiding reading, as Ms. James is doing. Guided reading gives the teacher the opportunity to observe individual students' particular struggles so that her or she can develop a strategy for improvement.

(Easy) (Skill 8.2)

78. In order to get children to understand specialized vocabulary, they can use:

    A. Newspapers

    B. Internet resources and approved Web sites that focus on their special interest

    C. Experts they can interview

    D. All of the above

Answer: D. All of the above

The answer is "D" because all of the responses are correct. There is not enough time for students to learn the enormous vocabulary in only one class so the teaching of vocabulary related to a particular subject is a very good way to help students understand the subject better.

(Average) (Skills 8.3)

79. **When a student uses sticky notes to make comments or ask questions while reading a book, they are using the following reading comprehension strategy:**

    A. Text structure

    B. Graphic organizer

    C. Textual marking

    D. Summarization

Answer: C. Textual marking

Students interact with the text as they read by inserting questions or comments regarding specific sentences or paragraphs within the text. Textual marking helps students to focus on the importance of the small things, particularly when they are reading larger works (such as novels in high school) and gives students a reference point on which to go back into the text when they need to review something.

(Easy) (Skill 8.4)

80. **Which of the following is an example of a synthesis question according to Bloom's taxonomy?**

    A. What is the definition of_____?

    B. Compare _____ to _____.

    C. Match column A to column B.

    D. Propose an alternative to_____.

Answer: D. Propose an alternative to_____.

There are six levels to the taxonomy: Knowledge, Comprehension, Application, Analysis, Synthesis, and Evaluation. Synthesis is compiling information together in a different way by combining elements in a new pattern or proposing alternative solutions to produce a unique communication, plan, or proposed set of operations or to derive a set of abstract relations.

(Easy) (Skill 8.5)

81. **How can DVDs be used in instruction?**

    A. Students can use DVDs to create pictures for reports

    B. Students can use DVDs to create a science experiment

    C. Students can use DVDs to record class activities

    D. Students can use DVDs to review concepts studied

Answer: D. Students can use DVDs to review concepts studied

The teacher's arms are never long enough to render all the help that is needed when students are learning new concepts and practicing skills. Audiovisual aids such as DVDs extend her arms. Students who need more time or instruction to master a skill can have that without having to work with the teacher one-on-one.

(Easy) (Skill 9.1)

82. **What might be a result if the teacher is distracted by some unrelated event in the instruction?**

    A. Students will leave the class

    B. Students will understand the importance of class rules

    C. Students will stay on-task longer

    D. Students will lose the momentum of the lesson

Answer: D. Students will lose the momentum of the lesson

The teacher who can attend to a task and an extraneous situation simultaneously without becoming immersed in either one is said to have "with-it-ness;" this ability is absolutely imperative for teacher effectiveness and success because it prevents students from becoming sidetracked.

(Average) (Skill 9.2)

83. **How can student misconduct be redirected?**

    A. The teacher threatens the students with extra homework

    B. The teacher assigns detention to the whole class

    C. The teacher stops the activity and stares at the students

    D. The teacher effectively handles changing from one activity to another

Answer: D. The teacher effectively handles changing from one activity to another

When the teacher effectively transitions from one activity to another, students know what to expect and are thus not easily sidetracked. The constant momentum resulting from smooth transitions keeps students focused on the task at hand.

(Rigorous) (Skill 9.2)

84. **Marcus is a first grade boy of good developmental attainment. His learning progress is good in the first half of the year. He shows no indicators of emotional distress. After the holiday break, he returns much changed. He is quieter, sullen even, tending to play alone. He has moments of tearfulness, sometimes almost without cause. He avoids contact with adults as often as he can. Even play with his friends has become limited. He has episodes of wetting not seen before and often wants to sleep in school. What approach is appropriate for this sudden change in behavior?**

A. Give him some time to adjust after the holiday break

B. Report this change immediately to administration; do not call the parents until administration decides a course of action

C. Document his daily behavior carefully as soon as you notice such a change; report to administration in the next month or so in a meeting

D. Make a courtesy call to the parents to let them know he is not acting like himself

Answer: B. Report this change immediately to administration; do not call the parents until administration decides a course of action

Any time a child's disposition, attitude, or habits change significantly, teachers and parents need to seriously consider the existence of emotional difficulties. Emotional disturbances in childhood are not uncommon and take a variety of forms. Usually these problems show up in the form of uncharacteristic behaviors. All stressful behaviors need to be addressed, and any type of chronic antisocial behavior needs to be examined as a possible symptom of deep-seated emotional upset. In a case where the change is sudden and dramatic, administration needs to become involved.

(Average) (Skill 9.2)

85. **What is a sample of an academic transition signal?**

A. How do clouds form?

B. Today we are going to study clouds.

C. We have completed today's lesson.

D. That completes the description of cumulus clouds. Now we will look at the description of cirrus clouds.

Answer: D. That completes the description of cumulus clouds. Now we will look at the description of cirrus clouds.

Transitions are language bridges between one topic and another. The teacher should thoughtfully plan transitions when several topics are going to be presented in one lesson to be sure that students are carried along. Without transitions, sometimes students are still focused on a previous topic and are lost in the discussion.

(Average) (Skill 9.3)

86. **What should the teacher do when a student is tapping a pencil on the desk during a lecture?**

A. Stop the lesson and correct the student as an example to other students

B. Walk over to the student and quietly touch the pencil as a signal for the student to stop

C. Announce to the class that everyone should remember to remain quiet during the lecture

D. Ignore the student, hoping he or she will stop

Answer: B. Walk over to the student and quietly touch the pencil as a signal for the student to stop.

If the teacher acknowledges inappropriate behavior, it can embarrass the student and provoke further misconduct in retaliation or encourage attention-seeking behaviors. An effective method for redirecting misconduct is to silently signal to the student that the behavior is inappropriate without stopping the flow of instruction.

(Rigorous) (Skill 9.3)

87. **What is one way of effectively managing student conduct?**

    A. State expectations about behavior

    B. Let students discipline their peers

    C. Let minor infractions of the rules go unnoticed

    D. Increase disapproving remarks

    Answer: A. State expectations about behavior

    The effective teacher makes clear, concise statements about what is considered appropriate and inappropriate behavior in the classroom, making sure to clearly outline the consequences for inappropriate behavior. It is helpful to prominently display classroom rules once they have been explicitly discussed.

(Rigorous) (Skill 9.3)

88. **Why is punishment not always effective in managing student behavior?**

    A. It tends to suppress behavior, not eliminate it

    B. It focuses on the negative, rather than the positive

    C. Students may comply out of fear rather than a genuine behavior change

    D. All of the above

    Answer: D. All of the above

    When punishment is the first and only strategy in behavior management plans, it may be misused to the point where it is no longer effective.

    Punishment tends to suppress behavior, not eliminate it. Punishment focuses on the negative rather than positive behaviors. There is also the chance that the child will comply out of fear, stress, or tension rather than a genuine behavior change. The use of social skills instruction, prompts, modeling, and reward systems in addition to punishment will yield the biggest changes in student behaviors.

(Average) (Skill 9.3)

89. **Robert throws a piece of paper across the room. The teacher ignores Robert. What is the teacher demonstrating?**

    A. Punishment

    B. Extinction

    C. Negative practice

    D. Verbal reprimand

Answer: B. Extinction

When a teacher uses extinction, reinforcement is withheld for an unacceptable behavior. This would not be a suitable strategy for serious misbehaviors where others are in danger of being hurt.

(Average) (Skill 9.3)

90. **To maintain the flow of events in the classroom, what should an effective teacher do?**

    A. Work only in small groups

    B. Use only whole class activities

    C. Direct attention to content, rather than focusing the class on misbehavior

    D. Follow lectures with written assignments

Answer: C. Direct attention to content, rather than focusing the class on misbehavior

Students who misbehave often do so to attract attention. Focusing the attention of the misbehaver as well as the rest of the class on the real purpose of the classroom sends the message that misbehaving will not be rewarded with attention.

(Rigorous) (Skill 9.3)

91. **What is most likely to happen when students witness a punitive or angry desist?**

    A. Respond with more behavior disruption

    B. All disruptive behavior stops

    C. Students align with teacher

    D. Behavior stays the same

Answer: A. Respond with more behavior disruption

When the teacher becomes angry, several things happen. Students feel that the one who made her angry has achieved his or her goal by misbehaving. They also feel that the teacher is not in control. Because the teacher has become emotional, students feel that they may also react emotionally. Students tend to sympathize with the target of the teacher's anger.

(Easy) (Skill 9.3)

92. **What can be measured utilizing the following types of assessments: direct observation, role playing, context observation, and teacher ratings?**

    A. Social skills

    B. Reading skills

    C. Math skills

    D. Need for specialized instruction

Answer: A. Social skills

Social skills can be measured using the listed types of assessments. They can also be measured using sociometric measures, including peer nomination, peer rating, and paired-comparison.

(Rigorous) (Skill 9.3)

93. **What increases the likelihood that the response following an event will occur again?**

    A. Extinction

    B. Satiation

    C. Verbal reprimands

    D. Reinforcement

Answer: D. Reinforcement

If a child misbehaves and his peers laugh, the behavior has been reinforced and is likely to happen again. The teacher needs to stop misbehaviors before they start when at all possible. However, the same principle applies with appropriate behavior. The teacher can influence repetitions of the behaviors she wants by reinforcing them when they occur. She can also create circumstances where she has an opportunity to reinforce good behavior.

(Average) (Skill 9.3)

94. **Why is praise for compliance important in classroom management?**

    A. Students will continue deviant behavior

    B. Desirable conduct will be repeated

    C. It reflects simplicity and warmth

    D. Students will fulfill obligations

Answer: B. Desirable conduct will be repeated

The tried-and-true principle that behavior that is rewarded will be repeated is demonstrated here. If other students laugh at a child's misbehavior, he will repeat it. Similarly, if the teacher rewards the behaviors she wants to see repeated, it is likely to happen.

(Rigorous) (Skill 10.1)

95. **When planning instruction, which of the following is an organizational tool to help ensure that you are providing a well-balanced set of objectives?**

    A. Using a taxonomy to develop objectives

    B. Determining prior knowledge skill levels

    C. Determining readiness levels

    D. Ensuring that you meet the needs of diverse learners

Answer: A. Using a taxonomy to develop objectives

The use of a taxonomy, such as Bloom's, aids teachers in providing instruction at a variety of levels.

(Easy) (Skill 10.3)

96. **What should be considered when evaluating textbooks for content?**

    A. Type of print used

    B. Number of photos used

    C. Whether it is free of cultural stereotyping

    D. Outlines at the beginning of each chapter

Answer: C. Whether it is free of cultural stereotyping

While textbook writers and publishers have responded to the need to be culturally diverse in recent years, a few texts are still being offered that do not meet these standards. When teachers have an opportunity to be involved in choosing textbooks, they can be watchdogs for the community in keeping the curriculum free of matter that reinforces bigotry and discrimination.

(Average) (Skill 11.1)

97. **Which of the following could be an example of a situation that could have an effect on a student's learning and academic progress?**

    A. Relocation

    B. Abuse

    C. Both of the above

    D. Neither of the above

Answer: C. Both of the above

There are an unlimited number of situations that can affect a student's learning. Students usually do not have the same tool box that adults have to deal with the feelings of anxiety and may require some additional guidance.

(Average) (Skill 11.1)

98. **Andy shows up to class acting aggressively and irritably. He is often late, sleeps in class, sometimes slurs his speech, and has an odor of alcohol. What is the first intervention to take?**

    A. Confront him, relying on a trusting relationship you think you have

    B. Do a lesson on alcohol abuse, making an example of him

    C. Do nothing, as it is better to err on the side of failing to identify substance abuse

    D. Call administration, avoid conflict, and supervise others carefully

Answer: D. Call administration, avoid conflict, and supervise others carefully

The first responsibility of the teacher is to ensure the safety of all of the children, including taking action if the teacher believes a student is abusing drugs or alcohol. Avoiding conflict with the student who may be using drugs and obtaining help from administration is the best course of action.

(Average) (Skill 11.1)

99. **A sixteen-year-old girl who has been looking sad writes an essay in which the main protagonist commits suicide. You overhear her talking about suicide. What do you do?**

    A. Report this immediately to school administration and talk to the girl, letting her know you will talk to her parents about it

    B. Report this immediately to authorities

    C. Report this immediately to school administration or make your own report to authorities if required by protocol in your school and do nothing else

    D. Just give the child some extra attention, as it may just be that that is all she's looking for

Answer: C. Report this immediately to school administration or make your own report to authorities if required by protocol in your school and do nothing else

A child who is suicidal is beyond any help that can be offered in a classroom. The first step is to report the situation to administration. If your school protocol calls for it, the situation should also be reported to authorities.

(Rigorous) (Skill 11.1)

100. **You are leading a substance abuse discussion for health class. The students present their belief that marijuana is not harmful to their health. What set of data would refute their claim?**

    A. It is more carcinogenic than nicotine, lowers resistance to infection, worsens acne, and damages brain cells

    B. It damages brain cells, causes behavior changes in prenatally exposed infants, leads to other drug abuse, and causes short-term memory loss

    C. It lowers tolerance for frustration, causes eye damage, increases paranoia, and lowers resistance to infection

    D. It leads to abusing alcohol, lowers white blood cell count, reduces fertility, and causes gout

Answer: B. It damages brain cells, causes behavior changes in prenatally exposed infants, leads to other drug abuse, and causes short-term memory loss

The student tending toward the use of drugs and/or alcohol will exhibit losses in social and academic functional levels that were previously attained. He may begin to experiment with substances. The adage, "Pot makes a smart kid average and an average kid dumb," is right on the mark. There exist not a few families where pot smoking is a known habit of the parents. The children start their habit by stealing from the parents, making it almost impossible to convince the child that drugs and alcohol are not good for them. Parental use is hampering national efforts to clean up America. The school may be the only source for the real information that children need in order to make intelligent choices about drug use. It's important to remember that if children start using drugs early, it will interfere with their accomplishing developmental tasks and will likely lead to a lifetime of addiction.

(Average) (Skill 11.1)

101. **Jeanne, a bright, attentive student, is in first hour class, English. She is quiet, but very alert, often visually scanning the room in random patterns. Her pupils are dilated and she has a slight but noticeable tremor in her hands. She fails to note a cue given from her teacher. At odd moments she will act as if responding to stimuli that aren't there by suddenly changing her gaze. When spoken to directly, she has a limited response, but her teacher has a sense she is not herself. What should the teacher do?**

    A. Ask the student if she is all right, then let it go as there are not enough signals to be alarmed

    B. Meet with the student after class to get more information before making a referral

    C. Send the student to the office to see the health nurse

    D. Quietly call for administration, remain calm, and be careful not to alarm the class

Answer: D. Quietly call for administration, remain calm and be careful not to alarm the class.

These behaviors are indicative of drug use. The best thing a teacher can do in this case is call for help from administration.

(Easy) (Skill 11.1)

102. A parent has left an angry message on the teacher's voicemail. The message relates to a concern about a student and is directed at the teacher. The teacher should:

   A. Call back immediately and confront the parent

   B. Cool off, plan what to discuss with the parent, then call back

   C. Question the child to find out what set off the parent

   D. Ignore the message, since feelings of anger usually subside after a while

Answer: B. Cool off, plan what to discuss with the parent, then call back

It is professional for a teacher to keep cool in the face of emotion and respond to an angry parent in a calm and objective manner. The teacher should give herself time to cool off and plan the conversation with the parent with the purpose of understanding the concern and resolving it, rather than putting the parent in his or her place. Above all the teacher should remember that parent–teacher interactions should aim to benefit the student.

(Easy) (Skill 11.1)

103. Which of the following should *not* be a purpose of a parent–teacher conference?

   A. To involve the parent in their child's education

   B. To establish a friendship with the child's parents

   C. To resolve a concern about the child's performance

   D. To inform parents of positive behaviors by the child

Answer: B. To establish a friendship with the child's parents

The purpose of a parent–teacher conference is to involve parents in their child's education, address concerns about the child's performance, and share positive aspects of the student's learning with the parents. It would be unprofessional to allow the conference to degenerate into a social visit to establish friendships.

(Easy) (Skill 11.1)

104. Mr. Brown wishes to improve his parent communication skills. Which of the following is a strategy he can utilize to accomplish this goal?

   A. Hold parent–teacher conferences

   B. Send home positive notes

   C. Have parent nights where the parents are invited into his classroom

   D. All of the above

Answer: D. All of the above

Increasing parent communication skills is beneficial for the student, the teacher, and the parents of the students. All of the listed strategies are methods a teacher can utilize to increase his skills.

(Average) (Skill 11.1)

105. Bobby, a nine-year-old, has been caught stealing frequently in the classroom. What might be a factor contributing to this behavior?

   A. Need for the items stolen

   B. Serious emotional disturbance

   C. Desire to experiment

   D. A normal stage of development

Answer: B. Serious emotional disturbance

Lying, stealing, and fighting are atypical behaviors that most children may exhibit occasionally, but if a child lies, steals, or fights regularly or blatantly, these behaviors may be indicative of emotional distress. All stressful behaviors need to be addressed, and any type of chronic antisocial behavior needs to be examined as a possible symptom of deep-seated emotional upset.

(Easy) (Skill 11.1)

106. Tommy is a student in your class; his parents are deaf. Tommy is struggling with math and you want to contact the parents to discuss the issues. How should you proceed?

A. Limit contact due to the parents' inability to hear

B. Use a TTY phone to communicate with the parents

C. Talk to your administrator to find an appropriate interpreter to help you communicate with the parents personally

D. Both B and C

Answer: D. Both B and C

You should never avoid communicating with parents for any reason; instead you should find strategies to find an effective way to communicate through various means, just as you would with any other student in your classroom.

(Average) (Skill 11.1)

107. According to recent studies, what is the estimated number of adolescents that have physical, social, or emotional problems related to the abuse of alcohol?

A. Less than one million

B. One to two million

C. Two to three million

D. Over four million

Answer: D. Over four million

Due to the egregious behavioral problems encountered in the teenage world today that have nothing to do with substance abuse, but mimic its traits, discrimination is difficult. Predisposing behaviors indicating a tendency toward the use of drugs and/or alcohol usually are behaviors that suggest low self-esteem. Such might be academic failure, social maladaptation, antisocial behavior, truancy, disrespect, chronic rule breaking, aggression and anger, and depression. The student tending toward the use of drugs and/or alcohol will exhibit losses in social and academic functional levels that were previously attained. He may begin to experiment with substances.

(Average) (Skill 11.1)

108. A child exhibits the following symptoms: a lack of emotional responsiveness, indifference to physical contact, abnormal social play, and abnormal speech. What is the likely diagnosis for this child?

A. Separation anxiety

B. Mental retardation

C. Autism

D. Hypochondria

Answer: C. Autism

According to many psychologists who have been involved with treating autistic children, it seems that these children have built a wall between themselves and everyone else, including their families. They do not make eye contact with others and do not even appear to hear the voices of those who speak to them. They cannot empathize with others and have no ability to appreciate humor.

(Rigorous) (Skill 11.2)

109. Mrs. Peck wants to justify the use of personalized learning communities to her principal. Which of the following reasons should she use?

A. They build multiculturalism

B. They provide a supportive environment to address academic and emotional needs

C. They build relationships between students, which promotes lifelong learning

D. They are proactive in their nature

Answer: B. They provide a supportive environment to address academic and emotional needs

While personalized learning communities achieve all of the goals in the answer choices provided, the most important goal is to provide a supportive environment to help address the academic and emotional needs of the students.

(Easy) (Skill 11.2)

110. Johnny, a middle-schooler, comes to class uncharacteristically tired, distracted, withdrawn, and sullen and he cries easily. What should be the teacher's first response?

A. Send him to the office to sit

B. Call his parents

C. Ask him what is wrong

D. Ignore his behavior

Answer: C. Ask him what is wrong

If a teacher has developed a trusting relationship with a child, the reasons for the child's behavior may come out. It might be that the child needs to tell someone what is going on and is seeking a confidant, and a trusted teacher can intervene. If the child is unwilling to talk to the teacher about what is going on, the next step is to contact the parents, who may or may not be willing to explain the child's behavior. If they simply do not know, it is best to seek a professional physician or counselor.

(Average) (Skill 11.3)

111. What is an effective way to prepare students for testing?

A. Minimize the importance of the test

B. Orient the students to the test, telling them the purpose of the test, how the results will be used, and how it is relevant to them

C. Use the same format for every test are given

D. Have them construct an outline from which to study

Answer: B. Orient the students to the test, telling them the purpose of the test, how the results will be used, and how it is relevant to them

If students know ahead of time what the test will be like, why they are taking it, what the teacher will do with the results, and what it has to do with them, the exercise is more likely to result in a true measure of what they've learned.

(Rigorous) (Skill 11.7)

112. The data coordinator of the district who is concerned with federal funding for reading will probably want to start aggregating scores immediately because:

   A. The public has a right to know

   B. By aggregating, the individual scores can be combined to view performance trends across groups

   C. This will help the district determine which groups need more remedial instruction

   D. Both B and C

Answer: D. Both B and C

Both choices B and C describe the role of a data coordinator within the district.

(Easy) (Skill 13.1)

113. When a teacher wants to utilize an assessment that is subjective in nature, which of the following is the most effective method for scoring?

   A. Rubric

   B. Checklist

   C. Alternative assessment

   D. Subjective measures should not be utilized

Answer: A. Rubric

Rubrics are the most effective tool for assessing items that can be considered subjective. They provide the students with a clearer picture of teacher expectations and provide the teacher with a more consistent method of comparing this type of assignment.

(Rigorous) (Skill 14.1)

114. Maria was an outstanding student in her elementary school in Brazil. Now she is nervous about starting fourth grade in the United States, although she learned English as a second language in Brazil. She and her parents should be relieved to know that:

   A. She will get extra help in the United States with her English

   B. There is a positive and strong correlation between a child's native language and his or her learning of English

   C. Her classmates will help her

   D. She will have a few months to study for the reading test

Answer: B. There is a positive and strong correlation between a child's native language and his or her learning of English

Research shows that the better handle a student has on his or her native language, the more easily he or she can acquire a second language.

(Average) (Skill 14.1)

115. Safeguards against bias and discrimination in the assessment of children include:

   A. Testing the child in standard English

   B. Requiring the use of one standardized test

   C. Using evaluative materials in the child's native language or other mode of communication

   D. Requiring that tests be issued by a certified, licensed psychologist

Answer: C. Using evaluative materials in the child's native language or other mode of communication

The law requires that the child be evaluated in his native language or mode of communication. Using a licensed psychologist to evaluate the child only meets the criteria if it is done in the child's normal mode of communication.

(Easy) (Skill 14.1)

116. Which of the following is an accurate description of ESOL students?

   A. Remedial students

   B. Exceptional education students

   C. Not a homogeneous group

   D. Confident in communicating in English when with their peers

Answer: C. Not a homogeneous group

Because ESOL students are often grouped in classes that take a different approach to teaching English than those for native speakers, it's easy to assume that they all present with the same needs and characteristics. Nothing could be further from the truth. Their backgrounds and personalities should be observed just as with native speakers.

(Easy) (Skill 14.1)

117. What is one of the most important things to know about the differences between first language (L1) and second language (L2) acquisition?

   A. A second language is easier to acquire than a first language

   B. Most people master a second language (L2), but rarely do they master a first language (L1)

   C. Most people master a first language (L1), but rarely do they master a second language (L2)

   D. Acquiring a first language (L1) takes the same level of difficulty as acquiring a second language (L2)

Answer: C. Most people master a first language (L1), but rarely do they master a second language (L2)

One of the most important things to know about the differences between first language (L1) and second language (L2) acquisition is that people usually will master L1, but they will almost never be fully proficient in L2.

(Rigorous) (Skill 14.1)

118. **Etienne is an ESOL student. He has begun to engage in conversation that produces a connected narrative. What developmental stage for second language acquisition is he in?**

A. Early production

B. Speech emergence

C. Preproduction

D. Intermediate fluency

Answer: D. Intermediate fluency

Attaining total fluency usually takes several years, although the younger the learner, the shorter the time it takes.

(Average) (Skill 14.2)

119. **Which of the following describes the functional approach to language acquisition?**

A. Focus on communicative elements

B. Focus on conceptual purposes

C. Focus on grammar elements

D. All of the above

Answer: A. Focus on communicative elements

In the functional approach to language acquisition, students learn practical, functional phrases rather than words in isolation. For example, young children might learn colors, letters, and numbers, while travelers may learn restaurant words, bathroom words, and other travel-related words.

(Rigorous) (Skill 14.2)

120. **Is it easier for ESOL students who read in their first language to learn to read in English?**

A. No, because the letter-sound relationships in English are unique

B. Yes, because this will give the children confidence

C. No, because there is often interference from one language to the next

D. Yes, because the process is the same regardless of the language

Answer: D. Yes, because the process is the same regardless of the language

Answer A is incorrect because literate ESOL students master the letter-sounds in English as well as native speakers do. Answer B does not hold true for all students. Answer C is incorrect because while there may be some interference in oral language, this does not usually happen in reading.

XAMonline.com

Finished with your Professional Education test? Interested in additional subject areas?

XAMonline has over 25 state-aligned FTCE titles on everything from Biology to Physical Education. These guides offer a comprehensive review of the core test content and include up to 125 practice test questions.

Featured Title:

FTCE General Knowledge

Prepare for your FTCE General Knowledge test with this state-aligned guide that reviews all of the current competency areas including: Mathematics, English, Reading, and Writing. Each section includes sample questions with full answer rationales to test your knowledge and ensure you understand the content. From analyzing the validity of arguments in reading to interpreting algebraic expressions, this guide will help you attain certification success the first time.

Additional FTCE Titles:

Art Sample Test K-12
Biology 6-12
Chemistry 6-12
Earth/Space Science 6-12
Educational Media Specialist PK-12
Elementary Education K-6
English 6-12
English to Speakers of Other Lang. K-12
Exceptional Student Ed. K-12
FELE Florida Ed. Leadership
French Sample Test 6-12
General Knowledge
Guidance and Counseling PK-12
Humanities K-12

Mathematics 6-12
Middle Grades English 5-9
Middle Grades General Science 5-9
Middle Grades Integrated Curriculum
Middle Grades Math 5-9
Middle Grades Social Science 5-9
Physical Education K-12
Physics 6-12
Prekindergarten/Primary PK-3
Professional Educator
Reading K-12
Social Science 6-12
Spanish K-12

Find XAM on

f t

XAMonline.com

300+ titles • FREE diagnostic tests • Study and test tips • Additional resources

Teaching in another state? XAMonline carries 14 other state-specific series including the GACE, NYSTCE and MTEL. Also check out our 30+ Praxis titles!

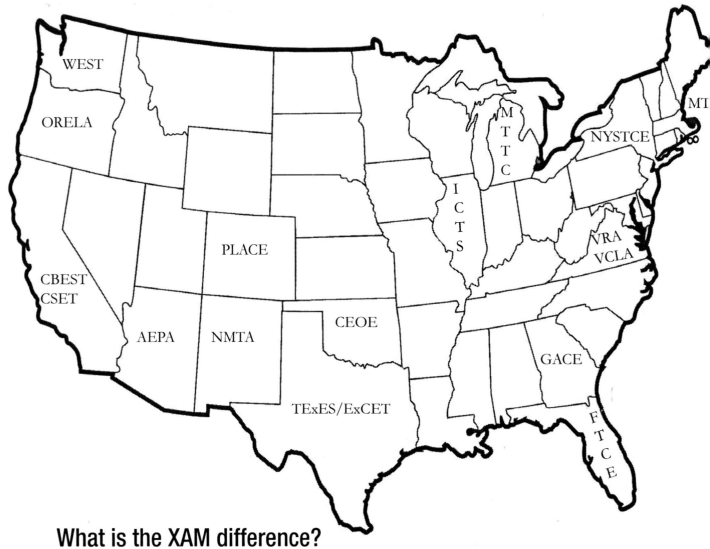

What is the XAM difference?

- State-aligned, current and comprehensive content
- Reviews all required competencies and skills
- Practice test questions aligned to actual test in both number and rigor level
- Questions include full answer rationale and skill reference for easy, efficient study
- Additional resources available online: diagnostic tests, flashcards, timed and scored practice tests and study/test tips

CPSIA information can be obtained at www.ICGtesting.com
Printed in the USA
LVOW09s2300240414

383196LV00001B/21/P